Disciples Who Make Disciples

HONEST QUESTIONS
REAL ANSWERS

Bruce Stopher

Seven Servants, LLC

SAN ANTONIO, TEXAS

Seven Servants, LLC

10730 Potranco Rd. Ste 122, Box 187

San Antonio, Texas 78251

www.sevenservants.com

Book Layout ©2019 BookDesignTemplates.com

Ordering Information:

Disciples Who Make Disciples: Honest Questions, Real Answers / Bruce Stopher. —1st ed.

ISBN 978-1-7334701-0-0

Contents

*Dedicated to
My army of sons
On three continents
Who are being disciples
And are making disciples*

Therefore go and make disciples of all nations, baptizing them in the name of the Father and of the Son and of the Holy Spirit, and teaching them to obey everything I have commanded you. And surely I am with you always, to the very end of the age.".

–MATTHEW 28:19-20

Acknowledgments

As strange as this may seem, my first acknowledgment goes to someone that I've never met; Joe from New York City (I'm not listing his full name because I did not get written permission to use his name). Joe was a featured presenter at a writer's conference that I watched online. Joe told a story about speaking to teenagers and not having enough time to answer their questions. He gave out his email address and asked them to send questions to him. Joe promised to answer each email. He then took those questions and answers and simply edited them into a book.

As I listened to Joe, I realized I've been answering a lot of questions about being a disciple and making disciples for years. Only 24 hours after watching that webinar, an outline of this book began to develop. I was so excited I couldn't sleep. And five months later, the completed book is in print. Thanks, Joe, for setting me on this path!

Second, I want to acknowledge a spiritual son, Josh Thomas. He lived in my home for two years. We struggled together through college and seminary classes, both finishing our degrees from Liberty University at the same time. When he moved out and got married, we continued to meet and began to talk about writing projects (beyond university!). Josh has served as an accountability partner for my writing. He asked questions, reviewed content, and provided critique and encouragement. Several of the questions covered here are from him. He provided a significant influence on the final shape of the book.

Third, I want to express thanks to two men who have influenced me over my lifetime. Cecil Bean was working as an education counselor at Fort Knox, Kentucky. He invited me to a Bible study, where I came to Christ three weeks later. He continues to check on me, having visited me at my home again this summer.

Phillip "Skip" Gray has also had an influence on my life. Even though we never lived in the same place for more than a couple nights! I remember driving Skip around during a conference. As we talked, he learned that I was a medical writer. He told me I needed to write a book about making disciples. No matter what excuse I threw at him, he pressed the point that there needs to be a fresh voice on an old topic.

Bruce Stopher   November 2019

Introduction

This book is different (like me!). I'd say it's more like the Bible than other books. What I mean is that you don't have to start at the beginning and go through to the end. When I lead someone to Christ, I usually ask him to begin reading the Gospel of Mark. I asked him not to start at the beginning. I know he might make it through Genesis. But Leviticus and Numbers are waiting down the road to confuse him.

So, like the Bible, though not as the inspired Word of God, you can start in this book wherever you want. This book is answering questions that you may have or not. See a problem that you've been stuck on for a while? Go there first. Feel free to read any chapter in any order. There are a couple chapters that refer to a previous one. Go backward if that helps you. I want to give you the freedom to do it your way. Make this book serve you, instead of you serving it.

However (there's always an exception to the rule, even in English grammar), it would be most helpful to you to understand what I mean by "disciple." Since there's a chance that we may not be on the same page there, at least not yet, it could be helpful to start there (that's chapter 8). That would be like starting in Mark's Gospel before getting into the letter to the Hebrews.

Let me address a couple "housekeeping details." In this book, my writing is geared toward men. The reason is simple. As a man, I disciple men. I will not disciple, mentor, or coach women. This goes back to the Billy Graham team's Modesto Manifesto. It also helps my writing and the understanding of many in my audience. Yet, the principles and answers you will read here apply to both women and men. Feel free to change the gender to a female orientation as you read![1] David Stoddard addressed this same thought in his book on

---

[1] When I went to nursing school, every book referred to the nurse as "she" or "her." What should you expect in a female-dominated work field? Even when I wrote papers, I referred to all nurses in the feminine. Now that I've finally broken that habit, I would prefer to stay in my own gender. As a fellow Christian, I hope you can give me a little grace here!

mentoring. He wrote in the masculine voice, he also said, "The principles—the big ideas—apply equally to both genders."[2]

As you read through this book, you may notice that I repeat a story or two; I tell you the same thing more than once. This is no mistake for two reasons. The first is that I just wrote that you can begin to read wherever you want. I make no assumptions that you will read every question and answer piece. The second reason is that I tend to repeat myself whenever I talk face-to-face with other men. Even the Apostle Peter seemed to have a habit of repeating himself (2 Peter 1:12-15).

While this book will spend a portion of its pages examining what the Scripture says about being a disciple who makes disciples, this is not an "academic" book. What I mean by that is that it has been written in everyday language – mine! People who know me personally know my "voice" – how I tend to talk, at a table, face-to-face with someone. While I can be considered a teacher, my approach is not that of an authority standing in the front of the room with "students" listening. That actually makes me laugh since historically, Jewish disciple-making looked precisely like that with a rabbi and his students.

I will write to you in the first and second person (I and you, me and we). Only when I am talking about someone else will I speak in the third person. I also write in "plain English." What I mean by that is you'll find simple sentences, words with three or fewer syllables, and in the active tense. This will not be like a college paper written to an intellectual audience. Intellectuals, though, are most definitely welcome to read the book and practice the ideas contained here.

You will also notice that I wrote this book with a "familiar" view. One of my reviewers called it "folksy." I've written things the same way as if we were talking together. This is the way I talk. That's part of giving you real answers to your honest questions. My answers come as if we were sitting together at Starbucks. When someone asks a question, they're looking for a real solution. They're not looking for a sermon (or a 20-page chapter of a book). So, I will keep my answers reasonably short.

I have a strong relationship with many of the guys I sit with at Starbucks (among other places). Being an adopted Texan, I also tend to call many of them "son." So, occasionally, I may mention a spiritual

---

[2] David Stoddard, *The Heart of Mentoring: Ten Proven Principles for Developing People to their Full Potential* (Colorado Springs, CO: NavPress, 2003), 12.

son in my answers. These are the men that I have been investing in over the years: discipling, mentoring, and coaching.

I have been asked why I call them "son" and whether this is part of discipling them. There is often a parental bond that forms in these relationships, but there's also biblical precedence. Paul called Timothy his "child in the faith" (1 Timothy 1:2). Peter called Mark his "son" (1 Peter 5:13). And the paralyzed man was called "son" by Jesus, who probably had never met him before that (Matthew 9:2). I stand in good company!

Since I just gave you three references to Scripture passages, I should say this as well. I will refer to Bible verses throughout this book. In only a few instances will I quote an entire passage. Feel free to look up any verse in the translations of your choice. This book quotes mostly from the New International Version (NIV) since the translators are generous with their copyright permission.

There are other books written about making disciples. There are different spellings in each book, such as making disciples, disciple making, disciplemaking, and disciple-making. There is no agreement on the right terms. In this book, I will use making disciples, disciple-making, and disciple-maker*. If I'm quoting someone else, I'll use the words he did. The Chicago Book of Style doesn't help us much here! As I wrote this book, I brought portions of it to a writer's critique group for review. Most of the writers there were non-Christians. One of the things that confused them most was the difference between the local church and the Church. A few thought the Church referred to the Roman Catholic Church.

Because of this confusion, I put a glossary at the back of the book. The first time I use a term that is in the glossary, I will mark it with an asterisk (*). You can see that I did that with the term disciple-maker above. I won't use it in every answer because too many asterisks will spoil the broth (only the saying is "too many cooks")!

At the end of some of the answers (but definitely not most of them), you may find a subsection entitled *Making This Yours*. These are questions that I might ask you if we were sitting together talking about that subject. If you see one of these subsections there, process your thoughts on that topic. Set a goal if you need to. Talk about your ideas or aim with your small group. Or talk about it over coffee with another disciple. When other avenues don't work, you can always contact me through the Facebook Group *Disciples Who Make*

Disciples. If there's a question that you don't see in this book (I know there are a few outliers), you can also ask that question there as well.

My desire is that you will find real answers to honest questions. I want to see you growing as a disciple and who makes disciples. Let's do that together!

Section One

Being a Disciple

"If we are going to make disciples,
we need to know what that is."
– Jonathan Parnell [3]

We need a clear grasp of what a disciple is and does. You cannot be a disciple if you don't know what one is or does. It's impossible to make disciples if you don't know what you're making. This section answers fewer questions than the second section, but we need to start here. It's an absolute must!

No one sets out to make a car without knowing what a car is and what it's used for. How can we compare a 5-year-old drawing a picture of a car and a 40-year-old making a car in his garage? Yet, we would expect that the 5-year-old to become a 15-year-old who can drive. One day he might have enough skill to make his own car. Making disciples is not as hard as making a car. But to do either, you must know what it takes to get to the result.

To be clear about being a disciple, we must avoid circular thinking. I have asked countless people for a description of a disciple. It's been amazing how many have responded "a follower of Jesus." Then I ask for a description of a follower of Jesus. At least half of the answers come back as "a disciple of Jesus." That's classic circular thinking!

The main question in this section addresses the definition of a disciple. It will be the most extended answer in this book. So, I will split my response into seven parts.

There are six verses in the Gospels where Jesus talks about the traits of a disciple. (There are more when you count duplicate quotes in the Synoptic Gospels*.) Jesus does more than talk about these traits.

---

[3] "What Is a Disciple?" on Desiring God. Accessed on June 7, 2019 at: https://www.desiringgod.org/articles/what-is-a-disciple

He says *without* five of these traits, you cannot be a disciple. He goes on to say that *with* three other traits, you are a disciple.

I'm not making the first trait that I address a higher priority than the others. I take them in the order they appear in the Bible. Each attribute carries the same weight. You must possess all six to be a disciple. To go back to the car-making analogy, you need all the cylinders for your car to run well.

At a recent conference, I went to a breakout session on the theology of discipleship. A pastor asked the speaker how he could measure how his church was doing at making disciples. The speaker gave a vague, but common, answer, "Check to see how much they are like Jesus." On the one hand, this seems reasonable, although not very helpful. Definitely not measurable, which is what the pastor was looking for.

After the session, the pastor told me he felt like he was being set up for failure. None of us will ever reach the point where we are "like Jesus." At least not to the degree that the answer implies. Not on this Earth, at least. We know that won't completely happen until we reach heaven. So, if we can't make even one "complete" disciple in a lifetime here on Earth, have we been set up?

In the 1960s, Dr, Waylon Moore narrowed the scope for us when we wrote, "Christlikeness is the ultimate goal for a Christian. There must be more tangible intermediate goals, however, such as the application of God's word to spiritual conditions, consistent and effectual prayer, obedience to the Lord's revealed will, and witnessing of His grace to others."[4] These intermediate goals are not only less vague, but they also reflect the core traits of a disciple. And they are much more measurable than "be like Jesus."

Let's be clear. Jesus *did* command us to make disciples. And he expected us to accomplish that in our lifetimes. It's not a setup. We just need to know what we're doing.

The Apostles who were with Jesus during that time understood what he meant. Sure, they moped around for a while, and even went back to fishing, until the Holy Spirit descended and set their hearts on fire. But once that happened, they left their fishing nets again and got down to the business of making disciples across their known world. They sure didn't seem to feel set up.

---

[4] Waylon Moore. New Testament Follow-Up: For Pastors and Laymen (Grand Rapids, MI: Wm. B Eerdmans Company, 1963), 58.

You may, of course, add further to the traits of a disciple as you like. I'm giving you the minimum description, though most people should be significantly challenged by this minimum. If you do add anything, make sure that you include the clear words of Jesus as you obey his command. Stay away from fuzzy concepts. Just keep things simple enough so your disciple can repeat the process. That's what Jesus did!

Did you notice in that last paragraph I said, "*your* disciple?" Some people may say, "He's not my disciple. He's Jesus' disciple." That might sound quite righteous, but it's not responsible. Would a parent say something similar about who is responsible for the upbringing of a child? Making disciples is your responsibility. It's not a group project, and you can't blame the group for your failure.

Then, get on with it. Be a disciple. Then, make disciples who will also make disciples.

CHAPTER 1

How Can an Everyday Guy Be a Disciple?

What a great place to start! It's good to know what and where you want to be, rather than to assume. Here's a thought. When Jesus talked about being his disciples, he was talking to everyday people, not just the twelve guys chosen to be with him. And when he gave his last command to make disciples, he was talking to everyday men. These men had jobs, families, and responsibilities, yet Jesus called them to be his disciples. Being a disciple is for everyday guys, not just some elite group.

This question may arise when someone puts too much emphasis on any one part of being a disciple. Someone develops a program that requires a lot of time to study theology. We have materials that need as many as ten hours of study each week. Then we spend more hours discussing the materials. (Not to mention travel time.) Those time requirements tend to exclude the very people who want to be disciples. And focusing on God's Word, while important, is only one of the eight traits of being a disciple. (All eight traits are listed together in chapter eight.)

I met someone recently who attended a one-year discipling program right after college. His description sounded great. He was living in community* with a group of other men about the same age. They learned how to have daily personal devotions*. They shared what they were learning throughout the week. They memorized a Bible passage every week. They often memorized more from a sense of competition, so I'm told. They had scheduled times of solitude and fasting. And, of course, there was a weekly Bible study and large group meeting. They were learning many wonderful precepts. Sounds perfect, right?

After all these glowing program details, I asked my friend one critical question. How was he doing with this all these spiritual disciplines three years later? "Well, I try to have my quiet time at least two or three times a week," was his candid response. He couldn't remember most of the verses he had memorized, much less had he learned any new ones. He had not fasted since the program ended. And he was "too extroverted" to practice solitude.

What caused this change? The dreaded "everyday life." He felt there was no way he could keep up the pace that the program set. Of course not. What can we expect when we add a 40-hour workweek to a 12-hour-per-day discipleship program? Reality sets in, and life puts the whammy on us! There isn't that much time in anyone's day. Unless you happen to be in full-time Christian work. "Those people" often get paid to practice spiritual disciplines or can at least work them into their workweek!

Being an everyday disciple of Jesus will take small chunks of time every day. But not so much that you don't see your family several nights of the week.[5] You will need to be in the Word. With ample time for prayer. And for sharing with fellow believers. Each of these things can be done in small portions. You can be a disciple by investing in little things. After all, didn't someone once say that it's the little things the matter?

Some people talk about how Martin Luther prayed every morning. Most likely, you have heard the quotation that on busy days he prayed for two hours instead of one. Here's a news flash. Luther was an Augustinian priest. They were known for spending hours in prayer while fasting and confessing. My point is that prayer was something Luther did as part of his job. He was one of "those people" mentioned above. Pastors and other church leaders should always have more time to pray than everyday guys. Sorry, it's the honest truth.

There's no question that a disciple (the precursor for a disciple-maker) needs to have a handle on God's Word. That doesn't automatically equate to a seminary degree. There are thousands of seminary-trained men and women who do not "rightly handle" God's

---

[5] If you are gone from your family three or more nights per week for Christian activities, you may be in danger of "performance discipleship." That's a fancy, modern description for being a Pharisee!

Word (2 Timothy 2:25). We don't have to wait until we can pass a test to be confident with the Scriptures.

A disciple must *abide* in the Word (John 15:7), but the Bible gives us leeway on how we can do that. We can do what works best for us individually, and let others do what works best for them. We can choose to read, listen, study, or memorize – in any combination – any or all of these practices with the purpose of abiding in the Word.

There's only one thing beyond the eight traits (listed all together in chapter eight) you *must* do to be an everyday disciple. Stop comparing yourself to someone who doesn't have the same everyday as you do.

In the next six parts, we're going to see what Jesus said to two groups of people. There were twelve men that he called to be with him so he could send them out later. We'll call them full-time Christian workers. Then there were the multitudes. Thousands of people who Jesus called to be his disciples. And they kept their day jobs. My guess is that you're in this second group. That's why you ask questions like this; because being an everyday disciple is hard.

You can succeed at being an everyday disciple!

Making This Yours

Do a quick, realistic assessment of what's eating up your time on a daily basis – work, sleep, meals, family, church, fun, zoning out.

What must remain "as is" and what could be cut back (whether painful or not)?

CHAPTER 2

What is a Disciple? - Part 1 - Luke 14:26

"If anyone comes to me and does not hate father and mother,
wife and children, brothers and sisters—
yes, even their own life—
such a person cannot be my disciple."

As the first of six verses we will look at about being a disciple, this verse includes two things Jesus said about the traits of a disciple. It's important to note who Jesus was talking to. Luke says it was a large crowd that was "going along with Him" (Luke 14:25, NASB). The Greek word that Luke used here was *symporeuomai*. We can find that word used in other places by Luke and Mark. We can get a better understanding of this word by looking at the last time this word appears in Luke:

> "As they talked and discussed these things with each other, Jesus himself came up and *walked along with* them." (Luke 24:15, emphasis mine)

"They" were two men leaving Jerusalem by way of the road to Emmaus. Jesus came alongside them as they were walking and joined them. At that point, the two men didn't think they had anything in common with this fellow traveler. On this road, there was safety in numbers, and he might help them keep a good pace. There were at least seven miles to walk on Roman paving stones.

Back in Luke 14:25, we see there was a large crowd of people walking along with Jesus. We're not told the reason that they followed him. What were they attracted to? His teaching? Or his healing of people? Or even the meal he provided to thousands of others? Whatever the reason, it was in the presence of this multitude that Jesus begins to teach on being a disciple.

How does Jesus begin to describe one of his disciples? We find his opening words in Luke 14:26. "If anyone comes to me and does not hate father and mother, wife and children, brothers and sisters—yes, even their own life—such a person cannot be my disciple."

I've heard more than a few sermons on this verse. Yet, only once in London, England did I hear someone talk about the first phrase.[6] "If anyone comes to me." Take a moment to think about that. First, Luke writes that a large crowd was walking with Jesus. Then Jesus says, "If anyone comes to me." Isn't that precisely what they were doing? Or have we missed something?

The word Luke chose to use for "come" is *erchomai*. You can see this word is different from *symporeuomai* (walking along with). We can find this word *erchomai* in the New Testament over 600 times. The first time we find it is with the Magi in Matthew 2:2 ("we saw his star in the east and have *come* to worship him"). We find it last in Revelation 22:20 ("*Come*, Lord Jesus).

But this word "come" doesn't stand alone in Luke 14:26. Jesus says, "If anyone comes." Jesus is not assuming that everyone will come. If he did would might have said, "When anyone comes." So, there's a large crowd of people walking along with Jesus. It's as if he assumes that they won't all come, even as they are walking along with him.

Let's consider that the first step of being a disciple is that we have come to Jesus. But by using the word "if" (*ei* in Greek), Jesus is making an if-then type of claim. Try reading it this way: If you come to me, and hate others, then you will be my disciples. (We'll get to that word "hate" shortly).

Coming to Jesus does not make you a disciple, but it's a step in the right direction. It's the second half of Jesus' words that hold a defining trait of a disciple. Some churches teach that as soon as you come to Christ, you are a disciple. This flies in the face of what Jesus said here. And what he said, to be clear, is "he cannot be my disciple" by coming

---

[6] Whenever I'm in London, I love to attend the Metropolitan Baptist Tabernacle. It's the church where Charles Spurgeon preached. The messages at the Sunday evening services always encourage people to come to Jesus.

alone. If we only meet half of his statement, it's impossible to meet the whole.

Don't mistake what I'm saying. Coming to Jesus is essential. It's the first step toward being a disciple. But the coming doesn't make you a disciple any more than deciding to buy some paint makes you an artist. It's the attitude that Jesus says makes you one of his disciples.

So, let's get to that attitude. Jesus used the word "hate." That seems to go against the grain of everything we learned about gentle Jesus, meek, and mild.[7] Perhaps, though, you have heard a sermon that explains this "hateful" attitude. Almost everyone agrees that this word is comparative. What does that mean? Compared to what?

Compared to the love we have for Jesus, it seems, at least to some, that we hate other people. Here's a way to think about that comparison. You're having a conversation with your mom. She's got some ideas about what you should do. But you want to do something different. She looks at you and says, "What. Do you hate me?" Many of us may have experienced this. Your mom knows that you don't actually hate her (at least I hope so). But to her, you seem to be putting something else at a higher priority than her desires.

That's what Jesus is getting at in this verse. Not only have you come to him. Family or friends may want us to do something over and against what Jesus wants. As disciples of Jesus, we must choose what Jesus wants. Sometimes our own heart desires something different than Jesus wants. We must choose the Jesus option. (And the Devil says, "What do you hate me?" – no comparison meant between your mom and the Devil! And I'd probably have to tell the Devil that I do hate him!)

Your mother may invite you to come over for dinner. Most of us would go home for mom's cooking. However, if during dinner, Mom mentions how she thinks you spend too much time on Christian activities and not enough time with her, you may be forced into making a difficult decision. If we say "no" to mom, she's liable to get angry and accuse you of hating her. She might even stop making your favorite dinner! There's a choice we face between following Jesus and following mom.

---

[7] This descriptive title of Jesus comes from the first line of a poem written by Charles Wesley in 1742. But within that poem is the same idea of holding God's will, above all else: "Let me above all fulfill, God my heavenly Father's will." You can see the full lyrics at: http://www.hymntime.com/tch/htm/g/e/n/gentleje.htm accessed on August 19, 2019.

There can be other examples that might be closer to home for you. Parents who want you to go to college when you feel called to a one-year discipling program (Yep, I know that guy). Or a father who wants you to be a doctor or lawyer when you feel called to ministry (Yeah, that guy, too). Parents and other family members can often mean well in their desires for our future, yet if God is pointing in another direction, the disciple must follow God's direction and say "No" to any family pressures.

This is what Jesus is getting at with his call for you to hate your parents, siblings, spouse, children, and yourself. He gets first priority. And this will lead right into the next trait that Jesus holds for one of his disciples.

Making This Yours

When did you first come to Jesus?

Have you adopted the attitude of making Jesus' desires your own desires over and above the wishes of others? If so, how have you progressed in this attitude recently?

What is a Disciple? - Part 2 - Luke 14:27

"And whoever does not carry their cross and follow me
cannot be my disciple."

The very next verse in Luke ties the next trait of being a disciple to the previous one. To be clear, the word "and" does not begin the Greek sentence. But the oldest English versions insert it to make the connection clear to the reader.[8]

Here, Jesus adds two more traits for a disciple. The first trait is that he carries his cross. The Greek word for carry (*bastazō*) means "to bear what is very heavy or burdensome." A cross is a heavy burden, for sure. But there are not very many Christians today who are being hung on a cross. So how should we understand this?

It's interesting. Jesus talked about carrying a cross, and then he carried his own about a year later. His disciples didn't connect the idea of Jesus dying on a cross to this idea of carrying a cross. Peter argued that it would never happen (Matthew 16:22). And Matthew puts this verse right after Peter's "no way, no how" claim (Matthew 16:24).

---

[8] While this statement includes the King James version, I'm not speaking negatively about the KJV. The Wycliffe Bible inserted "and" over 100 years before James was even born. Even the Passion translation of 2017 makes this insertion.

Writing in the early 1700s, Bible commentator Matthew Henry tied these two ideas of death on the cross and carrying a cross together. Henry wrote some details about a man condemned to death by Rome. The man submitted to the sentence of death by carrying his cross. It was voluntary. He carried the cross willingly. That's not the picture we have in our minds, or the movies, when we think of this. Can you see the difference between carrying a burden willingly versus begrudgingly or out of a sense of duty?

Matthew Henry was someone who understood having a burden. His first wife died of smallpox. Henry married again, a year after his first wife died. The baby girl from his first wife died shortly after his second marriage. With a new marriage, a second child was born, but she died the next year. A third child was born and died the following year. Of his ten children, four died in infancy. All while Henry suffered from "sweats."[9] Yet, he continued to preach Christ in England.

We would have a hard time connecting to someone who lost a wife to smallpox or babies to measles. We often suffer from "first world problems." Limited time, broken dishwashers, the check engine light. And no one is getting the electric chair or lethal injection for their faith, at least not in America. It's hard to say what might be a real cross to bear today.

I would propose that today our burdens are those things that take us away from Christ. The average American Christian only attends church twice a month. In Europe, they only go once a month! Our attendance isn't prevented because of crops in the field or a broken buggy wheel. We're exhausted from our work week, and the kids need some attention – like a family outing.

It's hard to believe that going to church is now a burden. I cannot say what all your troubles are. For me, it included a wife fighting breast cancer for 12 years. I don't think we can fit all these things on a "burden scale." But, Jesus says we need to carry our own cross. Did you get that? Our own. Often, we're busy trying to figure out how to put our burdens on someone else's shoulders. But a disciple carries his own cross.

---

[9] It's not clear what the "sweats" were during the 1700s. In the 1500s, the sweating illness was a epidemic of unknown origin that killed thousands of Englishmen, but it wasn't reported after 1600. The "sweats" Henry suffered from may have been night sweats that had no known medical treatment.

There may come a time when the burden is too heavy for one person. It's the role of the local church to help each other with our burdens (Galatians 6:2). When my burden is light, I can step in and help you. Later, you may find the bandwidth to help me when I need it. It's the carrying of the burden that proves we are disciples. Ignoring the burden, neglecting the cross, that's another matter – but not the trait of a disciple.

I'm going to go slightly off the topic for a moment. Many American Christians seem, to least currently, to have a passion for alleviating poverty and human trafficking around the globe. At the same time, they seem to be oblivious to the needs of Christians around them. Perhaps we think that "the church" should help its own people – but *we* are the church!

As I was reviewing and editing this answer, one of my Christian friends from England contacted me with a need. Because he is HIV positive, the local church has rejected him even though he stopped living the lifestyle that gave him the virus. His family rejected him long ago. He is often alone and dependent on the care of others for basic needs. This is the kind of burden that someone cannot bear alone. While we consider the dire needs of the unbelieving world, we must also help with our own brothers and sisters.

Okay, I'll get off that soapbox!

There is a second trait of a disciple in this verse. Once we take up our cross, we then follow Jesus. With the burden; not without it.

I am reminded of Matthew 11:28-30, which says:

> "Come to me, all you who are weary and burdened, and I will give you rest. Take my yoke upon you and learn from me, for I am gentle and humble in heart, and you will find rest for your souls. For my yoke is easy and my burden is light."

We see some words that were in this and the above verse: come and burden. We must first come, take up the burden, and then follow. We can't follow Jesus if we haven't already come to him. And there's a burden involved in the following. It's a light burden. Maybe it doesn't feel that way right now. But as we gather with other disciples, we help carry each other's burdens.

But back to that word "follow." This is a popular word today. Many people identify themselves as followers of Christ. I would submit that this action alone does not equate to being a disciple. The verse we are currently considering says carry *and* follow. It's possible to follow Jesus in some manner, but not take up your own cross. If we shirk our cross, we simply aren't a disciple.

John 6:66 says, "From this time many of his disciples turned back and no longer followed him." These people heard some things that they felt were too hard, so they stopped following him.

There are times when things may become too hard. Burdens are tough. Yet Jesus calls us to carry our own burdens and follow him. A disciple does both. Jesus says if we don't do both, we cannot be his disciple.

Making This Yours

What is your burden?

How are you doing at carrying that cross?

Is there a burden that you are aware of that someone near you has?

CHAPTER 4

What is a Disciple? - Part 3 - Luke 14:33

"In the same way, those of you who do not give up
everything you have cannot be my disciples."

Here I go again by pointing out the obvious! The New International Version begins verse 33 with "in the same way." The New American Standard starts with, "so then." Either of these translations of the Greek *houtō oun* that Luke wrote will work. These terms function to connect verse 33 to the previous four verses (Luke 14:28-32), where Jesus gives two examples of what it looks like to count the cost. The first is a builder who needs to know the cost to finish his work. The second is a ruler who needs to know the cost of winning a war. Today we're probably most familiar with builders.

I first moved to San Antonio in the 1980s. Around that time, someone began building a 6-to-8 story building. They got the building permits and started clearing the land. The foundation went in, and then the steel beams went up. They were making good progress. We could see it step-by-step since the building was on a hilltop right off the highway.

Then something happened. Actually, nothing happened. The building process just stopped. Many of us wondered what the builder was doing. Were they were waiting for the right time, or for a specific product? But nothing happened, except silence.

The long silence was finally broken when the local newspaper wrote about the building project after people called in to ask about it.

They reported that the group funding the building ran out of money. Without money to continue, things simply couldn't go on. Over the next few years, the metal beams began to rust. The rusting red framework reached above the trees against the blue skies. No one could miss it as they drove past the site.

That rusty frame stood as a witness to someone who didn't count the cost of a project before starting. Even worse, those beams continued to rust for almost ten years. The owner didn't have enough money to finish the project. And he didn't have enough money to tear it down! Another news report said the tax office acquired the land for unpaid taxes, then auctioned it off to the highest bidder.

This is what Jesus was talking about in Luke 14:28-32. Most of us can think of an example like this. Of someone not finishing a project because they didn't know everything involved. There are failed businesses and building projects all around us, yet *most of us don't consider being a disciple a costly project.* Perhaps that's because the Western church has oversimplified the noble pursuit of being a disciple of Jesus.

In today's easy-breezy Christian life, we like words like grace, mercy, forgiveness, and freedom. We don't like "works" of any kind, and rarely do we hear about obedience. Yet Jesus is calling us to count the cost; to count the cost of following him above anyone else. And that cost is enormous—not easy-breezy!

The cost is everything. Don't give me push-back; Jesus said it! First, he went after how we relate to our loved ones (Luke 14:26). Then Jesus expects each of us to carry our own cross; to drag it along behind while following him. And now he goes after everything we own.

In Matthew 19:27, Peter says, "We have left everything to follow you!" When he says, "we," he's including all twelve of the disciples, including Judas Iscariot (verse 25). Why did Peter even say that? He was responding to Jesus telling someone to sell everything he had, give to the poor, and follow Jesus (verse 21).

But get this. Peter happens to mention that he and the others had left everything behind. But then he asks a question. "What then will there be for us?" Peter seemed to think that by leaving everything, there would be some kind of payoff later. That's not counting the cost, it's determining the return on investment – a business transaction. Not exactly what Jesus had in mind!

The builder expected to put up a building that would be a good source of income for years to come. But we shouldn't expect a payoff in this life. Jesus even mentions this idea in Matthew, chapter six. He says if you get noticed for your fasting, giving to the poor, or prayer you've had your reward already. He wants us to focus on laying up treasures in heaven, not here on Earth.

We see the earliest disciples do this in the Jerusalem church. They were selling personal things like plots of land. They then brought the money to the apostles to support their ministry and others in the church.

Many of you don't have land to sell. Look at what the rest of the church (non-landowners?) were doing: "All the believers were one in heart and mind. No one claimed that any of their possessions was their own, but they shared everything they had" (Acts 5:32). Did you catch that? They shared everything they had; everything usually means everything.

I'm not saying that you need to sell all your stuff. But you need to have an open-handed mindset. You need to know in your heart that it doesn't belong to you anymore. If you can't or won't count that cost, Jesus says, "You cannot be my disciple."

I've often heard of an analogy of thinking about everything that you own being in your hands. We offer all that we have by raising our palms up toward God. That sounds good, but you're still holding on to things. A rabbi once told me that it's more like offering it with your palms down – anything that sticks belongs to you!

In real life, we still own what we have. But we are stewards of what God has given us. If God calls to have it back, we need to be ready and willing to give it back. That's the heart of a disciple.

CHAPTER 5

What is a Disciple? - Part 4 - John 8:31

"To the Jews who had believed him, Jesus said,
'If you hold to my teaching, you are really my disciples.'"

In the Luke verses we looked at, it was our attitudes that Jesus addressed. These next three verses, from John's Gospel, involve our actions. Jesus' own brother wrote, "What good is it, my brothers and sisters, if someone claims to have faith but has no deeds?" (James 2:14).

You may wonder if this first verse from John fits better as an attitude. But it serves as the hinge between the attitudes and actions. There's an attitude involved in keeping hold of Jesus' teachings. But there's also an action expected. If we don't do both, we'll lose our grip.

This verse introduces when Jesus makes positive statements about being his disciple. The verses from Luke each ended negatively with "you cannot be my disciple." So, we've moved from if you *don't*, to if you *do* – it's all action from here!

These next three verses also only have one focal point, one trait to meet. The first two verses from Luke had two each. Having only one trait in each statement doesn't mean these are going to be any easier. These will take work; we'll need to be men of action! We can't get lost in our thoughts here.

Bible experts think at Jesus is teaching in the Jerusalem Temple when he says this (John 8:20). As you read the context (always a good thing to do), there seem to be different groups of Jews hearing him.

To be sure, there would have been Jewish leaders around since they worked in the temple. Most of those leaders did not appear to follow his teaching. But there are some, like Nicodemus in John chapter four, who did seem to believe his words.

Luke specifies that Jesus is now talking to the Jews who have already believed in him. They might have even considered themselves to be his disciples. That would be why he clarifies for them what it's like to really be one of his disciples.

As we saw in the Luke verses, being a disciple required someone to come to him and to follow him. We could understand that these Jews in this verse have already done that. Following might have looked different for them than other disciples. Not everyone is in the same situation (or boat, which is where the Twelve often were).

There seems to be some variation in following Jesus. Some can do it with abandon; others with caution. We know today that someone who becomes a Christian in a Muslim culture needs to be careful. They can't openly follow Jesus with Christian t-shirts and cross necklaces. To do so could lead to death. You may have seen or heard about the murder of Christians in the Middle East and Africa. Situations can be different for different disciples – and that includes what following may look like in certain circumstances. (Most of you reading this are not in those types of circumstances.)

Realize that the people Jesus was talking to here were *already* believers. They had already accepted his teaching. Now he is prodding them to *hold* on to that teaching.

So, what does it mean to "hold to my teaching"? Let's go back to the Greek word that Luke used. That word is *menō*. The NIV translates that as "hold." The NASB goes with "continue." The English Standard Version gives us "abide." And the ESV seems to be the winner this time![10]

I'm going to use something a little more in our current vernacular. *Stick to it!* When we make a commitment to do something, there can be a temptation to give up on it, especially when times get tough. But there's something greater that is pushing us to continue, to keep it up,

---

[10] The word *menō* has a very wide range of meanings: abide, continue, dwell, endure, be present, remain, stand, tarry. Bible translators choose different words in different situations to help our understanding. When talking about a place, people would stay (*menō*) there. When Jesus wants someone to be near him, he asks them to abide (*menō*).

to stick with it. That something could be our hope, a desire to be obedient, or the encouragement of others.

So, a disciple not only knows the teachings of Jesus but also sticks to them. There may be a temptation to "progress" in our faith. Someone may remind you that you're in "the 21st century." Some governments pass laws to force us to change. We saw this in the United States with cake bakers in Colorado and Oregon. Christian companies were told they must support a specific type of "contraception." Christians are being even more restricted by the Canadian legal system.

Yet, most of life is not regulated by governments. There are other things that make it hard to stick to decisions, like peer pressure or even our own laziness.

Some believers may try to wriggle around the hard things by being "red-letter" Christians. They feel they only need to hold to what Jesus said. If Paul, Peter, John, James, or Jude wrote it, they don't have to follow it. They may say that if Jesus didn't say it (recorded in red letters in some Bibles), then they don't have to do it.

None of Paul's writings would include red letters, except for one small quote in First Corinthians. But Paul did go to Jerusalem to make sure that what he was teaching was approved by the Apostles – the men who had heard everything that Jesus said. Not only did they give their approval, but Peter commended Paul's writings as Scripture (2 Peter 3:15-16).

In the next generation after Jesus' death, an apostle or people who knew an apostle discipled many of the church leaders. They made sure to check what we have in our New Testament. And to keep out what didn't belong there. Two thousand years later, some "theologians" question even the things attributed to Jesus. But we must hold on to them. With a tight grip![11]

---

[11] I do not plan on giving you a list of all the commands of Christ. I will provide some basic thoughts on commands in Part Two – Making Disciples. Jesus commanded us to teach those things to the people we disciple.

CHAPTER 6

What is a Disciple? - Part 5 - John 13:35

"By this everyone will know that you are my disciples,
if you love one another."

Many people consider love to be an attitude or feeling. You may have heard someone else say, "Love is an act of the will." A secular article on the Psychology Today website makes it a little clearer. "Love is an action verb. It requires sweat equity. There is no such thing a passive love."[12]

A simple search for "love" on the Blue Letter Bible website returns 348 instances of the word. There are several different Greek and Hebrew words, but in English, we translate them all to "love." You may have heard a recording of C. S. Lewis talking about The Four Loves. He explains the differences in the four Greek words that I cannot go into here.[13]

I will focus on the word that John wrote when he recorded what Jesus said. It was the night of his betrayal. Before that fateful event, he spent the evening with his closest disciples. As soon as Judas left the

---

[12] "Love is an Action Verb: Don't Wait for Love – Make Love" on Psychology Today. Accessed on June 30, 2019 at: www.psychologytoday. com/us/blog/the-intelligent-divorce/201303/love-is-action-verb

[13] Lewis's talks on the BBC radio about The Four Loves was also converted into a print book. I prefer listening to Lewis's own voice as he discusses these four words with his British accent! You should be able to hear it for free at: https://archive.org/details/TheFourLovesCSLewisPart3ErosSexualLove (Accessed on October 2019).

room, Jesus speaks to the faithful followers. That was when Jesus gave his new commandment: to love one another. That kind of love would let others know that they were his disciples.

This word love was the Greek word *agapē*. Much has been written and spoken about the power implied by this word. It isn't the love of a pizza, or a sunset, or a favorite song. It's a self-giving love that puts the needs of others above anything you would rather desire. You might want a pizza, but you surely wouldn't give your life to have one, even in Chicago.

After living in Germany for four years, there were certain foods that I grew to love and now deeply miss. On a recent trip back to Germany, I couldn't wait to enjoy foods that I only craved for decades. But I wasn't going to give my life away to get that. On the other hand, I now miss real jaeger schnitzel and red cabbage even more!

The night before he died, Jesus told his disciples to love each other more. More than they had loved anyone else in their lives. As an example of the depth of that love, he died for them less than 24 hours later.

Their start at loving others was a miserable failure. Only a few hours later, in a dark garden at the arrest of Jesus, they scattered like flies. A couple of them did follow at a distance, but then denied even knowing him. John was the only one of the twelve apostles recorded as being at the place where Jesus died.

When times get tough, the quality and depth of our love shows. The harder things get, the more likely we are to seek safe shelter. Safe is an important word in that last sentence. If we're seeking safety, there's a pretty good chance that we're not practicing *agapē* love. That kind of love is self-giving, with abandonment, intending for the best for the other person, even to our own detriment.

Here's a clincher. The four Gospel writers never tell us how well the apostles loved one another. There's also not a story that implies they didn't. Did they succeed? The Bible seems to be silent regarding those original Apostles, perhaps simply because the Gospels are about Jesus and the Apostles were secondary characters. On the other hand, there are examples of Paul's love for the Gentile churches that he founded.[14]

---

[14] Read 1Thessalonians 2:17-3:10 to see Paul's attitude toward this church with whom he only spent a few weeks before being forced to leave town.

About 150 years after the death of Peter and Paul, Tertullian implies that the pagans of Carthage were saying, "Look how they love one another." But if we read all of what he wrote, he was actually *hoping* that North African pagans would see Christians in that view. It doesn't seem like it was really happening.[15]

Let's face it. This command of Christ is one of the toughest we'll ever face. Try as we might, we seem to fail more often than not. Sure; there are times when we are good at loving others. Some people are easy to love. But others...

This command seems to be an expansion of the second of the great commands: to love your neighbor as yourself (Matthew 22:39). We like to remind each other that the Great Commandment to love God and love people should be our focus. Yet, our sinful selves often get in the way.

Difficult as it may be, this trait of a disciple still stands. We can't ignore it and claim to meet the profile of a disciple. And we can't let our poor performance rule out being disciples. Every disciple will have one or two traits in which he excels. And every disciple will have one or two with which he desperately needs help.

Part of loving one another is holding each other to the standards that Jesus set for us. Sure, we take the log out of our own eye first, but then we help our brothers with the speck in their eyes (Matthew 7:3-5). Some would say that loving people means accepting them warts and all. I've heard it said, "We're not in the wart removal business." But when someone is falling short, to not help them is not to love them.

Disciples will be known by their love of one another. If someone gets close enough to us, they should be able to see that love in action. If they can't see it, we need to recalibrate.

This trait of a disciple is the hardest one to reach. It requires the attitudes that we've looked at from the three verses in Luke. It requires that we keep our relationships in the right priority (Luke 14:26). It requires that we carry our own cross and follow Jesus (Luke 14:27). And it requires that we count the cost of following Jesus (Luke 14:33), which will include the cost of loving others.

---

[15] For more about Tertullian, see "See how these Christians love one another" on Christian History Institute. Accessed on June 30, 2019 at: https://christianhistoryinstitute.org/magazine/article/see-how-these-christians-love

I'm reminded of a day I was at lunch with a co-worker at the hospital where we worked. One of the "scary nuns" sat with us (my co-worker wasn't as afraid of her as I was). Sister Mary, who was a nurse manager in the hospital, saw a doctor walk in and said, "There's Dr. Smith. I hate him." My co-worker laughed and asked, "Sister, is there anyone that you love?" Sister bluntly said, "I hate everyone and everything; except God." How this woman was a nun and a registered nurse was beyond me. One thing I do know; she was lacking in the loving others department![16]

One other example from my personal life. The night before I would marry my wife, we were at the wedding rehearsal. The Army chaplain officiating also happened to be my bride's father. As we went through the wedding vows, he asked me, "will you," instead of "do you" promise to love. I explained to him that the question needed to be "do you," so I could say "I do."

My father-in-law said, "I don't care if you *do* or not. If you won't say 'I will' then you can't marry my daughter. In my confusion, he explained things to help me understand. He said I could stand before him and God and say "I do" at the wedding, but later decide that I didn't anymore. Saying "I will" would cover the wedding day and every day after, even when I didn't feel like I did.

Several years later, my wife and I had an argument – a real doozy! I was steaming mad (but I don't remember what it was about today). I just remember thinking, "I said 'I will,' because I don't right now." My father-in-law was right. That little word "will" forced me to take action at the moment.

Love is an act of your will. It's a decision to do something for someone else, even at a cost to ourselves. Love is a trait of a disciple. One that we will chase for the rest of our lives.

This command to love one another seems to be the very last command that Jesus gave before his death. (The Great Commission came after his resurrection.) And just in case you didn't catch on to this idea here in John 13, Jesus will remind them again in John 15 – twice (John 15:12, 17)! When Jesus says something three times, we need to pay attention! And take action.

Love well, friends.

---

[16] I dearly love a lot of the nuns that I got to work with over the years. This particular nun was an exception to every other nun I have ever met, and the convent knew about her. They often lovingly approached her, but she would not submit to their correction. She eventually was removed from the order.

CHAPTER 7

What is a Disciple? - Part 6 - John 15:8

"This is to my Father's glory, that you bear much fruit,
showing yourselves to be my disciples."

By the time we get to this verse in John's Gospel, Jesus is in full teaching mode. The Apostles were together with Jesus in the Upper Room, where Jesus washed their feet. They had the Passover meal together. Jesus passed a cup of wine and some bread and told them to do this in remembrance of him. It was a solemn evening, that would get much worse in the garden across the Kidron valley.

These are some of the final words of Jesus before his crucifixion. I have heard Dr. Ed Stetzer, from Wheaton College, say more than once, "Jesus' final words should be our first priority." The focus of this passage of John's Gospel is on the disciples being connected to the vine and bearing fruit.

So, what did Jesus mean when he told them to bear fruit? Before you answer, put yourself in the sandals of those disciples. Within a few minutes, they will be walking from the upper room. They may have passed by a vineyard as they went to Gethsemane to pray. When they got to the garden, there were olive trees there.

At the time of Passover, the grapes would have been on the vine. Only fifty days after Passover, the grapes would be harvested. Olives, while not harvested until fall, would be blooming around this time. The entire way to the Garden of Gethsemane, the disciples had examples of fruit.

Jesus made it clear. A disciple bears fruit; much fruit. When he said this to his disciples in the upper room, they would have understood exactly what he meant. These disciples also came from Galilee, a very fertile agricultural area. Since most of us don't live in "farm country," we may not pick up the same ideas as the disciples did.

At a Bible study connected to my church, some college students considered what fruit looked like. One chirped up that it was obviously the fruit of the Spirit (Galatians 5:22-23). Everyone seemed to agree, and they started to move on to another verse. I pointed out that the disciples would not have thought this way. Paul didn't write his letter to the Galatians until at least twenty years later. We needed to take another stab at it and identify fruit from an agrarian context. The way first century people Galileans would have understood it, not twenty-first century urban dwellers who have a completely different context.

Since the year I became a Christian, I have heard the example of an apple tree. I had one in my backyard in southern Illinois, so I was familiar with them. When a tree has enough water and nutrition, it can bear leaves. When there's more nutrition than the leaves need, the tree will produce flowers. When the flowers get more than they need, the tree can produce apples.

If you provide ample water and care for an apple tree, it can produce hundreds of apples. One tree can produce up to 500 apples in a year. And they can produce for 15 to 20 years, providing up to 120,000 apples. Think of all the apple pie, apple crisp, apple butter— but wait!

Inside each apple are from five to twelve seeds. That's up to 6,000 seeds in a year from one tree! Or as many as 120,000 seeds over the life of the tree. If only ten percent of the seeds were to become new apple trees, it could result in 12,000 more trees with 120,000,000 apples!

This is an agricultural example of the multiplication process. In the old days, farmers held back part of their crops to use as seed for the next planting season. (Today, Western farmers tend to buy seed from a grower.) Even after selling ninety percent of their crop, they still have enough seed for another abundant harvest the next year.

The Great Commission is found in Matthew 28:19-20. It instructs us to produce disciples – in reproducing abundance. The eleven disciples took that command to make disciples very seriously. While they preached to both large groups, they made disciples the way Jesus did. Focusing on a small band of men; a band just like Jesus had around him.[17] The result was that within 300 years, there were Christians across the known world. That fruitful reproduction!

Disciples bear fruit; some will bear much fruit (Mark 4:20, where Jesus notes the different amounts). Not just leaves that look good, but people in whom their lives can be reproduced. Paul used the word "entrust" (ESV, NASB, and NIV) or commit (KJV). He wrote to Timothy, "And the things you have heard me say in the presence of many witnesses entrust to reliable people who will also be qualified to teach others" (2 Timothy 2:2).

If you look carefully, Paul had four generations in mind: Paul, Timothy, reliable men, others. That's not the only place where we see a focus on four generations. In the Old Testament book of Joel 1:3, we find, "Tell it to your children, and let your children tell it to their children, and their children to the next generation." The "you" is implied, that's one. Then your children (two), their children (three), and the next generation (four).

But just in case you need another four-generation example, here's what I think is the best one. John 17:4 reads, "I have brought you glory on earth by finishing the work you gave me to do." There's two; the Father to the Son. Then Jesus prays for his disciples, "My prayer is not for them alone. I pray also for those who will believe in me through their message" (John 17:20). That's two more; the disciples and those who will believe. That's spiritual multiplication. That's being fruitful; very fruitful.

Jesus said that the Father is glorified when we bear much fruit. The very first question in the Westminster Shorter Catechism is, "What is the chief end of man?" It then provides the answer, "Man's chief end is to glorify God, and to enjoy him forever."[18]

Our chief end is to glorify God. Jesus said that God is glorified "when we bear much fruit." So how can we not press into being fruitful and multiplying?

---

[17] A band of men doesn't have to have 12 or 13 members. An everyday disciple-maker may only have one or two men that he invests in. But if he bands together with other disciple-makers, the combined harvest can be significant.

[18] Westminster Shorter Catechism Project. Accessed on June 30, 2019 at: https://www.shortercatechism.com/resources/wsc/wsc_001.html

CHAPTER 8

What is a Disciple? - Part 7 - Putting It All Together

"Being a disciple of Jesus Christ is a lot different than just
going to church once or twice a week." – Tony Evans[19]

The six verses that we have looked at to answer the question "What is a Disciple?" should bring you to an agreement with Pastor Tony Evans. Being a disciple is much more than simply attending church often. Over the last six chapters, we have looked at several key attitudes and actions that Jesus said are clear traits of a disciple. He was so clear on these that he said these eight traits prove that you are or are not a disciple.

These traits begin with five attitudes:

- coming to Jesus,
- making him a priority,
- carrying your cross,
- following Him, and
- counting the cost.

Then from John's Gospel, we see that we must not only be familiar with the teachings of Jesus but also ensure that we abide in them. Two things should result from holding to Christ's teaching. We grow in

---

19 "Becoming a Disciple" on Tony Evans: The Urban Alternative. Accessed on June 7, 2019 at: https://tonyevans.org/becoming-a-disciple/

love with one another and that we bear much fruit. So, to add to the bullet points above, three actions that include:

- abiding in the Word
- loving one another, and
- bearing much fruit.

There are other traits we could use to define a disciple. Yet, the traits that come from the six verses we reviewed above give us plenty to pursue. Going back to the Tony Evans quote above, we could agree that many people are sitting in church who are not meeting many of these traits. Let alone other traits you may want to add. Years of church attendance, sermons, discipleship programs (the list goes on) do not, by themselves, result in people becoming the kind of disciples that Jesus expected.

To be fair, you may feel like you don't meet all these traits. You've got gaps, but then I know I do as well. The question we want to ask ourselves is whether we are moving in the right direction. Or are we just taking up space in a pew (I realize that many churches don't have these anymore, but you get my drift)?

As I think about these traits of a disciple, I must conclude that these are all indicators of a deep maturity in our faith. Perhaps you were "hateful" before you came to Christ (or even for some time afterward). But as you grew in your relationship with God, understanding his love and acceptance, you began to obey this new commandment that Jesus gave us. And as you continued to grow, the trait moved from something that you obeyed from a sense of duty to a character that became part of your personhood.

There must be a certain amount of time to bring maturity. A clear sign of maturity is fruitfulness. I have planted fruit or nut trees in every home I have ever owned. My current home has two oranges, two peaches, and one nectarine tree. When I planted those trees, they were already several years old. But I understood that they would not produce fruit immediately. My first orange tree had only three oranges the year after I planted it. The second year brought almost twenty oranges, but just last year (the fifth year), there were over a hundred. (Remember Jesus said that a disciple would "bear much fruit.")

I don't think there's a magic length of time that passes until you become a disciple. But a reasonable amount of time is necessary to reach full measure. Maturity doesn't happen overnight. It also shouldn't take twenty years. People around you should be able to see the traits that Jesus is manifesting in your life. If people can't see fruit, Houston, we have a problem!

In my little corner of the world, we use some terms to help us identify where someone is in their faith. A "convert" is someone who has recently developed a new life in Christ. A "young believer" is taking the beginning steps to develop his walk with Christ. He's learning God's Word, praying, begins to be in fellowship, which usually begins with church attendance.

An "emerging disciple" is in active pursuit of the traits of a disciple. Things might be messy here, but there's movement in the right direction, and he's progressed far beyond many of his fellow Christians in his church. And finally, a "disciple" has moved from pursuing the traits to becoming that person. You might say he's moved from pursuing to embracing.

While I describe these stages of being a disciple, let me address something that might be obvious or may have slipped by. Did you notice that the "young believer" is developing in his prayer life? None of the six verses that we examined mentioned prayer, and to take it a bit further, the only "spiritual discipline" mentioned was being in the Word.

I am not ignoring the importance of prayer or other spiritual disciplines, and I don't think Jesus was either. In fact, you'll notice that the attitudes and actions already mentioned cannot be accomplished without the use of spiritual disciplines, although they are not explicitly mentioned by Jesus.

One passage worth noting where Jesus does speak more clearly about them is Matthew 6. Let me take you there, which begins with Jesus saying, "Be careful not to practice your righteousness in front of others to be seen by them" (Matthew 6:1a). Jesus will go on to mention three spiritual disciplines – prayer (Matthew 6:5-8), fasting (verses 16-18), and giving to the poor (verses 2-4). Notice when addressing each of these spiritual disciplines, Jesus said, "when you." Jesus referred to these things as practicing righteousness, and he expected that his hearers were already doing these things.

The young believer, also referred to as a "child," is growing in spiritual disciplines that help him begin to know the Father (1 John 2:14a). No relationship develops overnight, based on a decision to know or follow (or both). Here again, time is critical to the development of a disciple.

How are you doing at embracing the traits of a disciple that we've discussed? There will always be one or two that you're strong in, and at least one that needs some work. Develop a plan to grow in that weak area over the next few months, while you strive to maintain the strong areas as well. If you're new to the idea of developmental plans, ask a disciple-maker for help.

Another question may have been stirred up while you evaluated these traits in your own life. What if you don't meet them? My answer is: Yes, you can disciple others while you're continuing to grow as a disciple yourself.[20] As if you ever stop growing as a disciple. There will always be room for improvement. Yet, there's no reason to sit on the sideline because you've got a flaw, although everyone sits on the sideline at a certain time during a football game. You can make disciples while you continue to grow as one – there I said it again!

---

[20] The first steps in making a disciple is called follow-up* (check the glossary for more). Following up a new believer and helping him begin his relationship with Christ can be done by anyone who is just a few steps ahead of the other person.

CHAPTER 9

Are the Words Disciple and Christian Synonymous?

"A disciple is one who follows Christ,
trusting in him alone for salvation,
worshiping his person, loving him with whole heart,
imitating his life, and obeying his teaching,
living dependently by abiding in Christ,
walking in the Holy Spirit, meditating on the word of God,
engaging in communion (prayer),
and partnering with the body of Christ (local church)
resulting in the transformation of the mind, the heart,
and the life and leads others to do the same."[21]
David Talley

What a loaded question! No matter how I answer this, someone might get offended. That's never stopped me from being honest in the past. And what a (long!) definition of a disciple from David Talley. His definition alone should separate the disciple from a Christian.

Here's the entire question as I heard it. "Is 'disciple' a synonym of 'Christian' in modern English? If not, what are the differences? Also, did language change over time to result in the current

---

[1] David Talley, "What Does It Mean to Be a Disciple and to Disciple Others? The Good Book Blog by Talbot School of Theology, May 9, 2016. Accessed on May 13, 2019 at: https://www.biola.edu/blogs/good-book-blog/2016/what-does-it-mean-to-be-a-disciple-and-to-disciple-others

meaning/understanding of the two words that some (including myself) use interchangeably?" Thanks to one of my spiritual sons for being brave enough to ask the question.

I was asked a similar question: "Are all believers disciples?" We might *want* to agree that the words Christian and believer are synonymous. So, without ignoring another spiritual son, I'll answer both questions, using the words of the first. But with two questions, it explains why I go into so much detail.

People do, in fact, use these words (Christian, believer, and disciple) as if they mean the same thing. By doing this, we imply that they are synonymous. My answer upfront is that they are not, and I will explain why.

For some background, let's look at the use of the two words in the Bible. In the Old Testament, the noun disciple only occurs in Isaiah 8:16 and 50:4 (as לִמּוּד or *limmuwd* when said using English). The noun means someone who has been taught or has learned. Or better understood, a learner. The verb (to learn) appears three more times (Isaiah 54:13; Jeremiah 2:24 and 13:23).

The Greek word for disciple is *mathētēs* (μαθητής) and appears only as a noun. Let me point out that today, we use a verbal form of the word – to disciple someone. Some nouns are also verbs. And some nouns have become verbs. I immediately think of the company name Google (a noun) and how we now google (the verb) something.

To the broader question's point, our language has changed over time. The noun "disciple" becoming a verb is a great example. Let's say that the words "disciple" and "Christian" are synonymous. Then why don't we ever "christian" someone (as a verb)?[22] We only disciple them. If we did use "Christian" as a verb, it would support the idea that the words are synonymous if we did. But then, sorry, we don't.

Back to the Greek word. Strong's concordance shows the word *mathētēs* appears 246 times in the New Testament. Over these 246 times, we find it in the Gospels 220 times and the 26 times in the book of Acts. Beyond Acts, the word never appears. Interestingly, Paul wrote several of his letters before Luke wrote Acts. It seems like the word was already falling out of usage.

---

[22] A verb that has fallen out of use is "christianize." It was first used in the 16th century. It meant to convert someone, sometimes by force. Most christianized people did not meet the traits of a disciple that we have discussed before.

There are only three places where the word "Christian" appears in the Bible (Acts 11:26; 26:28; and 1 Peter 4:16). That Greek word is *Christianos* (Χριστιανός). This builds on the root word *Christos* (Χριστός). We translate that to Christ in English, equivalent to the Hebrew word Messiah. You can compare that to the word *mathētēs* and see that they are nothing alike. So how did we start to use them as if they are alike?

Ignatius Theophorus (c. 50 – 108 A.D.) lived in Antioch of Syria into the early second century. Antioch was the same place where people were first called "Christians," although that was much earlier than Ignatius. It was Ignatius who began to tie together the words disciple and Christian. When he wrote that way, he meant that people could see your Christianity in the way you lived.[23] If your life doesn't set you apart from others around you, you're probably missing some key traits.

Justin Martyr (100-165 A.D.) was born a few years after Ignatius was martyred in Rome. Justin picked up on Ignatius' lifestyle thinking. He wrote, "Let it be understood that those who are not found living as He taught are not Christians—even though they profess with the lips the teachings of Christ."[24] With the persecution of Christians in full swing, Justin may have been expounding the thinking of everyday Christians.

Early Church leaders like Ignatius and Justin seemed to have a mission in life. They wanted to make sure people who said they were Christians, in fact, were. The measure was their lifestyle; a lifestyle different from non-Christians. These leaders were concerned about what Christians in their lifetimes believed in. Yet, the proof of that belief was how they lived their lives.

I have some single guys who live in my home. Currently, one of them is a young Christian. He comes from a Methodist background but is not practicing (as they like to say). I asked him if there was a difference between a Christian and a disciple. He immediately said, "Yes!" So, I asked him to explain.

He felt that being a Christian today meant adhering to a system of thought. That is a system of thinking that has its roots in the Bible. But

---

[23] Gerhard Kittel and Gerhard Friedrich. Theological Dictionary of the New Testament. Vol. IX. Trans. by Geoffrey Bromiley. (Grand Rapids: Wm. B. Eerdmans Publishing Company, 1974), 576.

[24] David Bercot. A Dictionary of Early Christian Beliefs. (Peabody, MA: Hendrickson Publishers, 1998), 128.

he thought a disciple was more. It was someone who was following another person. A disciple could follow Jesus Christ or Karl Marx. He felt the goal of a disciple was to become like the person he followed. This young believer reflected Justin Martyr's thinking without even knowing it!

Here's the clincher. Since my housemate saw a difference between a disciple and a Christian, I asked him which one he was. "I'm more on the Christian side," was his quick response. As we talked about how he might become a disciple, he knew that he needed to be in the Bible and in prayer.[25]

Consider whether there may be another reason the lines between these words are blurry. A quote from an Air Force chaplain may illustrate it better. She said, "Being a disciple is hard." She was right. It is hard! And in an age of easy-breezy living, we often look for ways to make things easier. But Jesus didn't do that.

It's interesting that non-Christians and many nominal Christians see these differences. There is at least a segment of Christianity that blurs the line between being a Christian and a disciple. Perhaps it's because we live in a culture where we don't like to leave someone out. Everyone gets a participation prize. Could this be what Jesus meant when he mentioned separating sheep from goats (see Matthew 25:31-46)? To the untrained, immature eye sheep and goats may look (and smell) very similar.

Please don't think that I'm saying a "mere Christian" will be condemned. There are areas in the Bible where things that look similar will turn out to be treated differently. Sheep and goats; wheat and weeds. This Matthew passage focuses more on what those who were separated were doing, not what they were believing.

It's not a matter of salvation. Yet, the Bible tells us there are rewards in heaven. We should be investing there. Most of us expect, or at least would like to hear, "Well done, good and faithful servant!" (Note that these words appear in the same chapter of Matthew as does the sheep and goats part.) I have a question for someone who asks whether these words are the same. "What is it about your life that would cause Jesus to say, 'Well done, good and faithful servant'?"

---

[25] There are some church leaders today who would argue that my housemate is not a Christian. I wouldn't necessarily disagree. He seems to be more of a "not-yet-Christian" who may one day become a disciple of Jesus. Until then, we talk, and I pray.

Our goal is two-fold: to be disciples and to make disciples. To do both, we must know the difference between a disciple and a "mere" Christian, even when others use the terms as if they mean the same thing. There's nothing wrong with helping people become believers. They must do that before they can become disciples. As Christians, we don't want to aim short of the goal: to become disciples who then make more disciples.

CHAPTER 10

What is Discipleship?

"The words disciple and discipleship are not only overworked,
they have come to mean whatever the user wants them to mean."
William MacDonald[26]

Another loaded question! After two seminary degrees, I can safely say
is that there is no agreed-on definition for the word "discipleship."
Ask ten people for a definition, and you're likely to get ten answers!
Most will have something to do with a classroom setting in the church.
I heard a quote once that the church is addicted to the classroom.

On the website GotQuestions.org, they define it this way:

> "Christian discipleship is the process by which disciples grow
> in the Lord Jesus Christ and are equipped by the Holy Spirit,
> who resides in our hearts, to overcome the pressures and
> trials of this present life and become more and more
> Christlike. This process requires believers to respond to the
> Holy Spirit's prompting to examine their thoughts, words and
> actions and compare them with the Word of God. This
> requires that we be in the Word daily—studying it, praying
> over it, and obeying it. In addition, we should always be ready
> to give testimony of the reason for the hope that is within us
> (1 Peter 3:15) and to disciple others to walk in His way."[27]

---

[26] William MacDonald. *The Disciple's Manual* (Port Colborne, ON: Gospel
Folio Press, 2004), 17.

[27] "What is Christian discipleship?" on GotQuestions.org. Accessed on
May 16, 2019 at: https://www.gotquestions.org/Christian-discipleship.html

The GotQuestions answer is only a sample of a common way of thinking. It starts with the premise that every Christian is already a disciple. As a disciple, he enters a "process" of growth, and the Holy Spirit equips him to become more Christlike. This implies that every new believer already is a disciple. But what about those six verses we already looked at? It would be rare that any new Christian meets the criteria of which Jesus spoke.

Notice also that the word "requires" appears twice in the GotQuestions quote. Being responsive to the Holy Spirit is required. As well as being in the Word every day.[28] And the term "process" seems to mean that you're not doing it very well yet. But the quote implies you already are a disciple. When did the disciple learn to do these things? As a non-believer? I contend that if you're not already doing the things listed as "required," you're simply not a disciple! (John 8:31)

I would point out that, based on the GotQuestions definition," no one other than the Holy Spirit seems to help you in the discipleship process. The Apostle Paul seemed to have a different thought on that. He wrote that God gave certain people to the local church to equip them (Ephesians 4:12-14). That's not to say that the Holy Spirit is not involved. But Paul's writing points out that something else is missing – other people.

No wonder there's confusion. The church uses terms that confuse themselves. Let's just leave the quote above where it sits. I prefer to use the word disciple-making, or variations of that because I want the outcome to be disciples who make disciples.

While there has been no universally accepted definition for the word "discipleship," I find Mark Dever's explanation of the difference between discipling and discipleship coming close to who I use the two words. He writes:

"Discipling is deliberately doing spiritual good to someone so that he or she will be more like Christ. Disciple*ship* is the term I use to

---

[28] Notice that there is not a Scripture reference for being "in the Word daily." It has only been in the last 200 years that most Christians had access to the Bible, much less were literate enough to read it. Statistics show that only 12% of the people in the world could read and write in 1820. (See "Literacy" by Max Roser and Esteban Ortiz-Ospina. Accessed on September 21, 2019 at: https://ourworldindata.org/literacy).

describe our own following Christ. Disci*pling* is the subset of that, which is helping someone else follow Christ."[29]

At least Dever's explanation differentiates between how I grow myself (discipleship) and how I help others grow (discipling), but it still leaves a lot of room for content that should be covered.

As I complete my final edit of this answer, I just heard one of the Apostles of the Church of Jesus Christ of Latter Days Saints talk about discipleship. In his explanation, discipleship is the process by which a Mormon performs that work of the church in order to attain entrance into the third heaven. Mormons are notorious at picking up evangelical terms, like discipleship and grace, but applying different meanings to the words. I supposed this gives me one more reason to use the term disciple-making.

---

[29] Mark Dever. Discipling: How to Help Others Follow Jesus (Wheaton, IL: Crossway, 2016), 13. Italics a from the original material.

52

CHAPTER 11

Where Does Accountability Fit In?

Many Christian men know about accountability. It means giving truthful answers to questions about habits in their lives. They can seek accountability at work or, more often, in their personal lives. At church, some small groups are called accountability groups, but many men develop these groups spontaneously. Employed men often meet in the early morning before they head to work. (I've never met a woman who was in an "accountability" group.)

Before 1990, the word accountability was rarely heard in church.[30] Today's use of the word began with the Promise Keepers men's movement, founded in 1990 by a college football coach. Seven years later, a million men gathered in Washington, DC. The movement's growth was impressive but short-lived. Promise Keepers is currently trying again to "reunite, rebuild, re-imagine, and inspire the heart of men towards integrity."[31]

How did Promise Keepers move men toward integrity? Groups spawned by Promise Keepers used a list of questions men asked each other. You can still find these online. Almost all the lists were less than ten questions. They could be covered in less than 15 minutes over

---

[30] The New Testament does mention people being held accountable by God during the Judgment, but the term wasn't used in popular Christianity until recently.

[31] See the About Us section on the Promise Keepers web page. Accessed on May 26, 2019 at: https://promisekeepers.org/promise-keepers/about-us/

coffee together. The last question usually asked if you just lied about one of your answers. Here's a list from a book by Chuck Colson:

1. Have you been with a woman anywhere this past week that might be seen as compromising?
2. Have any of your financial dealings lacked integrity?
3. Have you exposed yourself to any sexually explicit material?
4. Have you spent adequate time in Bible study and prayer?
5. Have you given priority time to your family?
6. Have you fulfilled the mandates of your calling?
7. Have you just lied to me?[32]

Accountability is part of discipling but asking questions alone doesn't make disciples. Many men joined these groups and asked each other questions. But there was little instruction on the central traits of being a disciple. The primary focus of Promise Keepers was faithfulness in marriage and family.

In making disciples, there is a mutual sharing of our basic practices. Men share what they get from their devotions. They share what they are praying about. And when one is struggling with finding the time to do these, the other person helps by asking questions. So, questions like those above are involved. We just don't tend to ask all those questions at once.

Accountability can look different in disciple-making. The list above focuses on some negative areas: compromise, lack of integrity, looking at porn, and lying. These things are part of the list of traits that Christians should "put off: found in Colossians 3:5-9. Disciple-making will focus on more of the positive behaviors. Things that we see in Colossians 3:12-17. Christians are to be transformed into the image of Christ. It helps to be accountable in those positive areas as well. Not to just clean up our acts.

I put a more substantial focus on these positive aspects because of Jesus' teaching in Matthew 12:43-45:

> "Now when the unclean spirit goes out of a man, it passes through waterless places seeking rest, and does not find it. Then it says, 'I will return to my house from which I came'; and when it comes, it finds it unoccupied, swept, and put in order. Then it goes and takes along with it seven other spirits more wicked than itself, and they go in and live there; and the

---

[32] Charles Colson, The Body: Being Light in Darkness (Grand Rapids: W Publishing Group, 2003), electronic copy.

last state of that man becomes worse than the first. That is the way it will also be with this evil generation." (NASB)

In this passage, something bad (a demon) "goes out of a man." The demon returns to find things "unoccupied, swept, and put in order." With plenty of unoccupied space, the demon returns with seven other spirits. Now the man is worse off than he was before. What happened here was that the man got rid of the bad. But he didn't put anything good in its place. Some of our accountability can have that same effect. We don't want to create a vacuum. We want to be filled with the Spirit!

There's another reason to focus on the positive. Psychologists have found that when we think negatively about something, we can strengthen that thing in our lives. If we see something tempting and say to ourselves that we won't get involved, we're still thinking about the temptation. That allows the very thoughts you're trying to avoid to become stronger – just from a negative perspective.

Instead, psychologists suggest that we should train our minds to switch from the negative to a positive thought. This is what King David does in Psalm 110: 9-11. To keep his way pure, David hid Scripture in his heart (memorized!). So, when that tempting thought comes around, have a verse that you can think about instead of the temptation. That's also what Jesus did when He was being tempted by the Devil (Matthew 4: 3, 7, and 10).

We need to hold men to account when discipling. Just not on purity, where most modern accountability spends all of its effort. We need to teach others how to develop healthy spiritual disciplines. As men grow in these things, there's less room for impure thoughts.

CHAPTER 12

How Does Being a Disciple Benefit Me?

We can answer this question in more than one way. It may mean what benefit do you get when helped by someone else? Or, it might have a more cynical post-modern source. One that asks, "What's in it for me?" Let's ask the first option, then go on to the second.

As we grow as disciples, someone may have come alongside each of us in the process. And he's probably a little further along than you are. Maybe quite a bit further. In the world of being and making disciples, we would call that second person a disciple-maker*. In another context, we may call that person a personal coach. Let's run with that second context for a moment.

A personal coach is someone that I contact (but he might approach me, as well). Maybe I want to lose weight or gain muscle. I look for a coach who can help me there. Perhaps I want to run a marathon. I look for a coach who has run marathons himself. And I will probably look for someone who already has the weight gain (in the right places) or has that runner's build.

My personal coach assesses where I am today and what it's going to take to get to my goal. He will set up a routine to help me reach my goal. He might also let me know if my goal is too small or too big.

He doesn't just confirm my goal and hand me an exercise routine. He's with me to make sure that I'm doing the prescribed exercise the right way. Once I've got it down, he may back off during the routine. But he's always there to check and make sure that I stick to the right form. He tells me when to increase my reps or add another exercise. He doesn't leave and check back at the end of the year.

A disciple-maker is like a personal coach. He already knows how to do the basics; those traits of being a disciple are evident in his life. He's been through the circuit, and he knows the practices that helped him reach the goal and can also help you. A coach's life shows the results of his own work, and he is most interested in your results. We wouldn't accept an overweight personal coach. And we shouldn't accept an undisciplined disciple-maker.

I won't have to pay for a disciple-maker like I would a personal coach. He will spend time with me because he values me. He also has a desire to obey Jesus' Great Commission. As he spends time with me, he gets to know my strengths and weaknesses. He knows where he can give me some slack, and where I need tight oversight.

And like a personal coach, a disciple-maker will add to the prescribed practices as you grow. He knows what you're able to do, even when you're not sure of yourself. He can give you that "coach talk" to spur you on.

One of the best benefits of having a disciple-maker come alongside you is the depth of growth that can occur in your own life. Your disciple-maker will push you when necessary and cheers you with every success. He might even change things up when you're having trouble. Who wouldn't want that kind of help?

Now on to the more cynical, postmodern side of the question: "What's in it for me?" It shouldn't surprise any of us that this question comes up. The Western world is rife with ideas that everything and everyone should provide for my pleasure. If it doesn't provide for my own satisfaction, it should be avoided. Mass media marketing is completely geared this way. And churches, unfortunately, have begun to pick up on that message as well.

A few decades ago, the answer to this type of question would have been about obeying Jesus Christ. Someone saw this question on my Facebook author page. He replied, "It brings you in alignment with our creator despite the potential earthly outcomes." Neither of these answers about obedience or alignment will please someone with a "what's in it for me" attitude. That's because the question is looking for a quick, satisfying result.

Jesus did have something to say about this quick result way of thinking. We find it in Matthew 6:1, which reads:

"Be careful not to practice your righteousness in front of others to be seen by them. If you do, you will have no reward from your Father in heaven."

The disciple is less concerned about this quick result. He's more concerned about hearing his master say, "Well done, you good and faithful servant." If this second option of the question is what you mean to ask, you won't like my next statement.

You may be trying to be a Christian in order to get some tangible reward in the here and now. There's a segment of the American church that is referred to as followers of the Prosperity Gospel. It tends to teach using Jesus for worldly gain. If you fit, loosely or snuggly, into the group, I strongly encourage you to examine where you stand as a follower of Jesus. Some people followed him for what they could get – maybe a free meal, a healthier life. But when the going got tough, they got going to something more satisfying (John 6:66).

Jesus was much more interested in the long-term outcome; the treasures that could be laid up in heaven. Being his disciple means that we begin to take on his values. His values included a heavenly reward based on obeying his commands. For no other reason than he demands it.

Hopefully, I haven't spoken to anyone who is holding this second option to the question. If I have, please consider the fruitlessness of your current pursuit. Let's follow the first option and get someone who will spur us on to be a disciple who makes disciples.

CHAPTER 13

Why Doesn't Someone Disciple Me?

Unlucky question number thirteen. Even hotels avoid this number. But I can say with a sense of confidence that's it's not just a case of bad luck. Nothing feels worse than feeling a need for spiritual growth, yet not having someone to help you. I think there are two primary reasons for this: you and the other guy. Let's tackle the other guy first.

I've had some young guys tell me that they are being discipled by an older man. When I hear that, I make a mental note to get some time talking to that older man. I'll take Tom as an example. I heard about what he was doing and asked to meet him for lunch.

After the usual small talk, I got around to mentioning that I heard he was discipling someone. I got a puzzled look. I clarified with the name of the guy who said it. A perplexed look was all I got back from him. Then Tom said, "Well, we've met together a few times. But I wouldn't call it discipling. I just shared a few simple ideas. Besides, no one has ever discipled me, so there's no way I could do that myself."

You have no idea how many times I've heard that same "I've never been discipled" comment. The concept of being a disciple and making disciples is fairly new in our culture. I remember in 1974 a lady at church asked me what I wanted to do when I got out of the Army. At that point, I had no idea what my next job would be. So, I said, "I just want to be a disciple, no matter what else I do." This sweet little church lady looked at me with sad eyes and said, "Honey, they're all dead." Back then, "disciples" meant the twelve men who walked with Jesus.

Today, being a disciple might refer to someone who has gone through church training. It might even mean someone who meets one-on-one with another person. But only after meeting one-on-one with someone *above* them. That idea disqualifies most men. At least in their own eyes. So, if you ask one of them to disciple you, you won't get the answer you were looking for.

I was talking to a singles pastor at my church one day. He wanted to see more of his guys become disciples. I knew where he was going and told him I didn't have the bandwidth to meet with more. So, we talked about what it would take to get other men in the church equipped to disciple these younger men.

The pushback for equipping older men came from two directions. The pastor responsible for "men's discipleship" didn't see the value of training men to help younger men. He felt they needed help in their marriages and at being a father. Important areas to be sure, but how did it become more important than making disciples?

The other type of pushback came from the older men themselves. With a full-time job and family and church small group, how would they have time to meet with another man? And how would they find the time to add a training class? Any excitement of discipling someone was snuffed out by the worries and cares of the world (Mark 4: 18-19).

This shows that Jesus' teaching that "the harvest is plentiful, but the workers are few" still applies today (Matthew 9:37). Every generation will have a shortage of Christian workers, a.k.a., disciple-makers. So, this shortage can affect you. And if that's the case, I have a few suggestions.

Search the Internet for a local Christian group that is committed to making disciples. You might find one at a local college campus. Some disciple-making ministries have a website where you can search your area. If you find one, ask to meet with a leader. Find out if he might be able to disciple you. If he can't, he may know someone who can.[33]

There could be someone "not so local." In the history of The Navigators, many older Nav staff would travel to help someone. Not only have I heard these stories, but I have also driven up to four hours away from my home to meet someone. You won't be able to meet

---

[33] Be aware that college campus ministries are often in great need of people to help serve the students. If you ask to meet with a campus ministry leader, offer to volunteer in exchange for the help you need.

face-to-face weekly. But phone calls or web meetings can augment a less frequent face-to-face meeting.

And when all else fails, go for "electronic discipling." What's that you say? Recorded messages, both audio and visual, can help you learn to be a disciple and make disciples. Cru (formerly known as Campus Crusade for Christ) and The Navigators both have online resources that can help. The Navigators also host Discipleship Library[34] where you can find thousands of audio messages on being a disciple and making disciples.

When I lived in Germany, I couldn't find anyone nearby to disciple me. I found books to read, messages to listen to, even a conference in Switzerland to travel to. I did this for two years until someone moved "close enough" for me to take a 45-minute train ride to spend time with them. In other words, find some source to meet your needs until something better might come along. But don't give up!

You might notice in the flow of this answer, I've begun to talk about *your role* in being discipled. Sometimes, it's not just that there's no one available to disciple you. More of the weight might rest on you. The last two paragraphs pointed out some resources you could try if there isn't anyone available. If there is someone available and they decline to disciple you, you may need to do an internal inventory. Maybe even ask the person who declined to meet you for some constructive criticism. If you do that, just listen and consider the value of this advice.

I have known several guys who complained that no one was discipling them. When I dug a little deeper, I found that availability was the issue. When disciple-makers are few, we may need to change *our* calendars to make space to be discipled.

One of my disciple-making friends, a married woman with six children, is willing to meet with other women. But, it needs to be in her home, while she's minding the children or cooking a meal. If you can "only" meet at Starbucks, she will simply decline the chance to meet you. (Nothing could be better than her teaching you how to walk with Christ amid a busy home.)

Being available is key to being discipled. If you want it bad enough, you may need to give up something else. The bank teller who first discipled me was available from 5:30 a.m. to 7:00 a.m. to meet. *On*

---

[34] See www.discipleshiplibrary.com

Saturdays! I didn't bat an eye. I was hungry enough to drag myself out of bed and get there in time to soak up everything he had to say.

Another barrier to being discipled that I've noticed lately has to do with the age of the disciple-maker. You might think that someone needs to be "old enough" to disciple you. Whatever that means. I've known guys who turned down a discipling relationship because the disciple-maker was only three years older than him. (The bank teller who discipled me *was* three years older than me!) It doesn't take a guy in his 80s to help you learn to be in the Word and develop your prayer life. He just needs to be a few steps ahead of you!

I also know guys in their 20s who won't meet with someone in their 60s (like me!). There's even an unspoken, but surely thought about, term that they use – "creepy old man." This might be the influence of the media or a parent saying out you can't trust older men. Age is no longer thought of as something that brings wisdom but danger. Even within the church! The newest generation of adults expresses a deep desire to be mentored. Yet, they have a tough time finding the "right" qualifications for the disciple-maker. (It reminds me of the story of Goldilocks and the Three Bears – too hard, too soft, too hot, too cold!)

This idea of who can disciple you comes down to the area of being teachable. Paul tells Timothy not to let others look down on how young he was (1 Timothy 4:12). That was probably written as much for the benefit of the church at Ephesus as for Timothy. Paul may have been aware of an attitude in the church that looked down on Timothy's teaching because of his age.

Being teachable is a highly important trait to be discipled. If someone is trying to invest truths and practices into your life, and you resist it, don't expect the relationship to go far. Be open to learning from someone who is already practicing the content. Being closed to learning – what we call unteachable – disqualifies you as a candidate. You might suspect this if someone meets with you a few times and then stops.

A third area that you need is to be faithful. 2 Timothy 2:2 says, "The things which you have heard from me in the presence of many witnesses, entrust these to faithful men who will be able to teach others also" (NASB). If you use the NIV, it reads "entrust in reliable men." The synonyms faithful and reliable should give you a good idea of what I mean here.

Discipling doesn't only happen in the time you're meeting with someone. Your disciple-maker might ask you to read something, look up some verses, or listen to a podcast or talk. A faithful man does what's being asked of him. Maybe something comes up that prevents you from doing it once or twice. But if you consistently don't get these little tasks done, your disciple-maker begins to question if you are faithful.

When I begin to meet with someone, I will often ask them to read a small pamphlet. It's always a small item that would take 10-15 minutes to get through. If it hasn't been read when we meet again, I encourage them to find time the next week. If this little task isn't done by the third meeting, there won't be a fourth meeting. I won't say I'm sorry either. There are too many guys out there that will be faithful to spend time trying to convince someone who isn't to be one.

Put together these three traits I talked about, and you get an acronym that helps you remember them – FAT. A FAT man is faithful, available, and teachable. If you don't have someone willing to disciple you, I suggest you evaluate how FAT you are. You don't need calipers or a weight scale.

Here's the difficult part. You may be missing one or more of the traits of a FAT man. You need to do some serious evaluation of that trait. I can tell you that you can't just flip a switch and the trait magically appears. You may need to do a Bible study – in depth.[35] I'm not aware of a printed study that covers these traits. It will take work on your own.[36]

And even beyond your own. You may need to talk with your small group about helping you develop in this trait. You might be able to talk with your pastor, as well. And sometimes, you may have significant difficulty in an area. You may need to speak with a biblical counselor for a few sessions to get a better understanding and a development plan.

I know a lot of disciple-makers who talk through the parable of the four soils (Mark 4:1-20). These disciple-makers draw a diagram of

---

[35] A "word" study uses Bible resources, like a comprehensive concordance, or the cross references that may be printed in your Bible. Search for a keyword like "teach" to see every use in the Bible. You can also look for biblical characters display the feature you are studying.

[36] I previously mentioned Discipleship Library (www.discipleshiplibrary.com). All three of these topics are listed with a page worth of messages available to listen to for free. Some even have a pdf file that allows you to take notes and think through the topic more deeply.

four quadrants – one for each type of soil. The objective is to try to encourage the hearer to be in "better soil" – the soil that yields a fruitful crop.

There are two problems with this approach. 1.) Jesus never implied that someone could move from rocky soil to good soil. And 2.) The parable is meant to teach one clear idea, not try to extract many thoughts from one story. The last thing we need to do is give someone a guilt trip that they're not good enough. Especially if that guilt trip is not based on clear biblical teaching.

If God speaks to you about an area of your life that you need to change, begin working on it. And it's okay to ask others for help with that. But be careful that you do not let a well-meaning person make you feel bad when you're not being fruitful to their standards.

How Many People Should I Be Discipled By?

This might sound like a strange question to some, especially if you are having trouble finding just one disciple-maker. It comes from places where discipling is more of a group activity. I know a church in the Pacific Northwest that has "DNA groups." DNA is an acronym for Discipleship, Accountability, and Nurturing. The thinking is that a small group of guys get together and disciple one another.

I am also aware of a discipling ministry at an Army post in Texas. They practice discipling others as a team approach. Three men team up to disciple one man, yet they meet with the man one-on-one.

It's also common for church leaders to talk about classes and groups created to disciple people in the church. Many of these groups use "discipleship" materials, chosen by the church to help fulfill the Great Commission.

You would think that with so many people being involved in "discipling" that there would be a lot of disciples coming out of the other end. Let me address why this doesn't seem to be happening, along with the results that I've seen from the three groups above.

DNA groups gather together as a cluster of three or four guys who are at the same stage of life. They've been Christians for about the same length of time. This means that they are "discipling one another" from a position of weakness. It's like a group of kindergarteners trying to teach one another not to write the alphabet. If at least one of them doesn't know how to *be* disciples, they won't become disciples in this process.

As I mentioned before, the team approach is a popular discipling style in some parts of the U.S. military. In this model, three disciple-makers meet with the same person on different occasions. (Military guys, at least the single ones, do have more time available when in the States.) There was a different problem in this group – lack of focus.

Each disciple-maker on the team works from his strength. Each of them meets with the same emerging disciple weekly or bi-weekly. When I asked them what the other two men were focusing on, I got a blank look. The reason I asked was that I had met one of these emerging disciples. He mentioned how confused he was with many topics being taught to him each week.

The third type of group is seen in a lot of church small groups and classes developed to provide discipleship. They've done Bible studies, watched videos, fed the hungry, and had tons of discussions. Each of these activities seeks to help make disciples. Or in church talk, "discipleship." As I write this, this morning, I heard a youth pastor talk about how walking through an airport as a group together was a "discipleship opportunity."

Before I get you totally upset, let me assure you that I find value in each of the activities mentioned above. However, I know that these things do not result in someone *being* a disciple. At least, not by themselves.

So, what does it take? A small group? A team of disciple-makers? One person? What? I'll start by saying all three options are useful – one-on-one time, small groups, and larger groups. Let me explain.

It should be obvious that one-on-one ministry was, in fact, occurring in the New Testament. Jesus did call twelve to be with Him. Yet there are plenty of times when Jesus was having a one-off talk with someone, often on a more intense, personal topic. Perhaps that talk was within earshot of someone else.

When Jesus asked Peter if he (Peter) loved Him (Jesus), it seems that John was nearby (John 21:20). That conversation was completely between Jesus and Peter. But done in a way that John not only heard it, but it was so memorable that he later wrote it down. We simply can't assume that Jesus didn't have one-on-one times with His men.

At the same time, several of those one-on-one times came out of small group times. We often see Jesus with three or four disciples during a teaching opportunity. Other times the full group of twelve is there. The Apostle Paul also had a group of twelve men he was discipling in Ephesus (Acts 19:7-9).

And of course, we see larger groups in the New Testament. Jesus was often teaching to a multitude (Matthew 5). Local churches gather together in large groups to pray and hear the Word. Conferences will also gather very large groups of Christians together for teaching.

All three of these methods (one-on-one, small group, and large group) help make disciples, but none of them can stand on their own.

There's not a church in the world, at least the free world, that doesn't have a large group meeting – most of them weekly. The Western church has recently embraced the idea of small groups. While we can trace small groups from the first century to today, that emphasis in most modern churches has only existed over the last 30 years. Yet in most churches, we can find very few people, if any, who are meeting one-on-one to grow as disciples.

I assume that you're already part of a local church and probably involved in a small group. That's standard fare. But if you're not meeting one-on-one with someone, you're missing out.

Let me expand on that. When I came to Christ, it was after a Wednesday evening small group Bible study. I had been there for three weeks, somewhat lost with what was going on. On April 14, 1974, I was asked what made me think I was a Christian. I was alone with one other fellow—one-on-one. My confused response led him to share the gospel, and me to pray. All on a dirt road in Kentucky.

The very next day, I attended a Maundy Thursday service at the chapel.[37] Several complete strangers came up to me and told me how excited they were that I had become a Christian. I was pulled into the larger group of the chapel community, continued to go to the small group Bible study, and met one-on-one with the man who led me to Christ.

It was during those one-on-one mornings together (our usual time to meet was 5:30 a.m.) where my disciple-maker explained a lot of things I did not understand. He knew I didn't know how to use a Bible or pray. He spent many-a-morning teaching me these basics.

I was (and continue to be) involved in large group church meetings and small groups Bible studies. Yet, I don't think I would have survived without my spiritual father discipling me. But he didn't

---

[37] Maundy Thursday is the Thursday before Easter when the Church believes that Jesus washed His disciples' feet and instituted the Lord's Supper. That night, He would be arrested and crucified the next day.

try to do everything himself. As a three-month-old believer, he introduced me to Ray. Ray started training me to share my testimony and the gospel. (Remember my story about the Army model of people teaching from their strengths.) Even so, I still had a primary disciple-maker while another man helped me in a specific area.

In the first six months of my new life, I learned to read and study my Bible, pray for myself and others, and begin to share my faith. My disciple-maker moved away right about then (something that happens a lot to military people). Another man then took the lead and picked up where the first left off. I found out later that my discipler organized that transition.

If you asked me at the one-year mark how many men discipled me, I would have answered (and still do) that there were three. But each was doing it in concert with the others.

When I moved to Germany, there was no one available to disciple me. So, the last guy continued to help me from afar. He mailed me cassette tapes (this was before the Internet and MP3s) that would help me develop. After two years, I heard that someone moved to a town "nearby." So, I started taking a 45-minute train ride to be discipled by him. And when I returned to America, I found another guy who would complete the discipling process for me. He was a three-hour drive away, but well worth it. I would still consider all three of those guys my mentors.

The person who led you to Christ should be the one who begins discipling you. He is your spiritual parent; you are his spiritual child. That might be a youth minister or college campus leader. Senior pastors may have a time problem discipling new believers. Billy Graham couldn't possibility disciple everyone who came to Christ at one of his crusades. So, he had Lorne Sanny and Charlie Riggs put together a training program for volunteers to begin discipling people who made decisions at crusades.[38]

We live in a world with an ever-increasing amount of mobility. That means there will often be more than one person who disciples you. There will be even more who equip, mentor, and coach you.

If more than one person is discipling you at the same time, there should be one who is the primary disciple-maker. Multiple disciple-makers can lead to tour confusion if they don't coordinate. While they

---

[38] "Remembering Charlie Riggs: Lifelong Laborer" published on July 21, 2008 by The Navigators. Accessed on May 19, 2019 at: https://www.navigators.org/charlie-riggs-lifelong-laborer/

are only talking about one thing, you are trying to apply too many things at once. (You may not have much control over that, but you can talk with your primary disciple-maker if you're getting overloaded.)

Each disciple has a strength and a weakness. You will pick up your disciple-maker's strength, but you can also pick up his weakness. You may not even know what that weakness is. But it will probably be something that the disciple-maker does not talk much about. Don't be afraid to ask if there is someone else who can help you with a specific area.

In every discipling relationship, there needs to be a movement toward the biblical definition of a disciple. That will focus on being in the Bible, developing an effective prayer life, learning to share your faith, growing in community with other believers, and being transformed into the image of Jesus Christ. That, most likely, will not all be done by one person.

CHAPTER 15

Should I Be More Than a Disciple?

Interesting question. By using the word "more," this might mean something like a church leader. Or it could imply that a disciple is only the beginning of a process. This might happen when we think that a new believer is already a disciple. I would hope that the seven answers to the question of What Is a Disciple would alleviate that confusion.

There is never a good time for someone to stop being a disciple. Even as a pastor or some other church leader, we never stop being a disciple. If we do, there's a problem. Whatever else we may become, we are first and foremost disciples.

My answer to this question, though, is a strong Yes! You should be more than a disciple. You should be a disciple-maker. Implied in the Great Commission is the need for being a disciple-maker. Part of fulfilling the Great Commission is teaching every disciple to obey all the commands of Christ. That would include the last command – to make disciples. If we stop at being a disciple, we have not fully met the command Christ gave us.

If you feel you meet the traits of a disciple, you're on a launching pad. You should continue to grow as a disciple as you continue to abide in God's Word and be increasingly more fruitful. But it's also time to begin to disciple someone else. To help a new believer begin to grow in the same things that you have now begun to master. Perhaps not a "new" believer. Some guys have been waiting for years for someone to help them grow.

Side Note: When you feel that you meet the traits of a disciple, it's always good to get someone else's view. There will often be areas of our lives that are less obvious to us. But these could be glaring to others. There's always room for continued growth as a disciple of Christ.

So yes, be more than a disciple. Become a disciple-maker. Even as that everyday guy that we talked about at the very beginning of this section. Be a disciple who makes disciples!

Section Two

Making Disciples

"Discipling others is the process by which a Christian with a life worth emulating commits himself for an extended period of time to a few individuals who have been won to Christ, the purpose being to aid and guide their growth to maturity and equip them to reproduce themselves in a third spiritual generation."[39]
-Allen Hadidian

Some personal friends read my answers before I completed publishing this book. In their remarks, there was a consistent thought. They wondered why I did not address the Great Commission in the first part of this book. I will give one simple response. Before you can make disciples, you must be a disciple.

Being a disciple, and continuing as a disciple, is the clear standard that Jesus called each of us to. These were things that he spoke about throughout his ministry on Earth. Yet, as Jesus left Earth for his heavenly home (at least until his glorious return), he left us with a command to make disciples of all nations. This next section answers questions about making disciples.

These questions and answers require us to understand the traits of a disciple (see chapters 2 through 8) and to possess those traits ourselves. We simply cannot make a disciple without being one already. We can't train someone to be a carpenter without first being a carpenter. It takes a doctor to make a doctor. Or whatever other examples you may prefer.

---

[39] Allen Hadidian, *Discipleship: Helping Other Christians to Grow* (Chicago: Moody Press, 1987), 45.

Do you have any outstanding questions about being a disciple? Then I strongly suggest you turn back to Section One and read the answers that can give you a better starting point. If you cannot find an answer to your particular question there, you can still get an answer. Join my Facebook group *Disciple-Making Questions* and post your question there. You can get answers from myself and other disciple-makers in the group.

At the same time, you do not need to have made high marks on a "disciple exam" to begin to disciple another. You only need to be a few steps ahead. As a matter of fact, I find that helping a younger believer solidifies several areas in my own life. It applies a type of peer pressure to stay on top of things.

By all means, get your questions answered here. If you have questions I didn't answer, I will invite you to find my *Bruce Stopher – Author* page on Facebook.com. From there you will be able to send me your question and expect an answer in a reasonable amount of time.

CHAPTER 16

How Do I Make Disciples with a Busy Life, a Family, and a Demanding Job?

The last section on *Being a Disciple* began with a question about being a disciple from an "everyday guy." This is another such question since an everyday guy tends to have a busy life, a family, and a demanding job. Is that all you've got? At least throw in your church volunteer work to make it seem even harder. (Just kidding; just kidding!)

There's a reason that I listed this question first in this Making Disciples section. That's because none of the answers that follow this one will matter if you think there's no room in your life to make disciples. We may often consider disciple-making the realm of professionals; those church leaders (a.k.a., pastors) who get paid to make disciples. After all, how many books about disciple-making do you know of that were *not* written by a pastor? (Speaking of pastors, make sure you check the pastors' responses in Section Three about disciple-making in the local church.)

There's a disconnect here. What professionals write about does not connect with how we see ourselves accomplishing those things. Whether it's true or not, we think of pastors sitting in an office writing sermons, making visits to the hospital, and sometimes even speaking at a wedding or funeral. What else could they possibly be doing? (Ask your pastor to find out!)

I understand that you're busy; that you rarely have time for the recommended weekly "date night" with your wife. I remember in the 1960s talking about all the future appliances that would come, along with computers, which none of us had yet to see. My teachers explained that these wonders would make our lives so easy that a full-time workweek would only be 20 hours. Somebody lied!

Hmm. Something about that last paragraph causes me to pause for a different topic. If you're "so busy" that you can't date your wife, you have a serious problem. Making disciples will be the least of your worries. You could, potentially, be making alimony and/or child support payments if you don't get with it. Totally off-topic, I know, but you simply must make your wife a top priority, even above the children.

Think about this with me for a moment. Jesus called his followers to a certain place for a planned meeting after the resurrection. Then he gives them the Great Commission (see the next question for more details). We know that at least Peter was married (how else do you have a mother-in-law?). That means Peter probably also had children. Most likely, most or all the eleven remaining Apostles also had families.

Peter had a family, a household to maintain, a fishing business, and responsibilities. What would have happened to the Great Commission if Peter said, "Once the kids are out of the house, I can do that"? Or, "Once I reach my retirement, I can do that." Where would you be in your faith today if Peter and the others didn't figure out how to do their part in making disciples?

Even the Apostle Paul maintained a "gig job." He was a professional tentmaker. We see him doing that while he was in Corinth (Acts 18:1-4) and probably in Thessalonica (2 Thessalonians 3:8). You might rationalize that things are different now. But we could also argue that everything's the same. New believers still need to be discipled. We, the everyday disciple-makers, are the ones that need to accomplish most of the work. Or, as I'm known to say, there simply won't be a next generation of disciples.

Most men will find two regular periods in their busy lives when they can actively make disciples. If you have a standard 8-to-5 job, that would be in the early morning and at lunch. Churches figured out a long time ago that the best time to get men together is early on a weekday morning. Churches may host a men's small group at a coffee shop or diner where men can grab breakfast or coffee. While they might offer groups for couples in the evening, men are targeted on a weekday morning. (The quarterly men's pancake breakfast on a Saturday being the outlier, but still in the morning.)

Lunches have a tighter time slot but are still useful. (Although military chaplains figured out that a "lunch and learn" was best for that crowd.) Hourly civilian workers may only get 30 minutes for lunch. For you, with that short of time, your discipling prospects will be with co-workers. Salaried workers can often take up to an hour, and that often allows you to leave the building. Meeting somewhere convenient between your two locations may work best. In either case, being aware of time constraints help us be intentional in our discipling.

Here are a couple ideas that might be helpful for you. For some guys who I meet with I set the timer on my mobile phone to make sure we get finished in time. I have also been known to pick up lunch and bring it to a job site to save time for the construction workers that I disciple.

These time limits are where I get the most pushback on the ability to meet with someone. We assume that there's just not enough time to make it valuable. Part of that assumption has its roots in church services or small group meetings. They all last at least an hour, some small groups can go more than two, without travel.

Let's see; how many times have you complained about how long the sermon is? How many times have you hinted that a business meeting should never last more than 30 minutes? Why then do we think that making disciples needs to be done in 60-minute intervals?

The other assumption is that a relationship requires large amounts of time to grow deeply. It is important to have a solid relationship with a disciple. But you don't have to spend oodles of time catching up on each other's kids and their activities when you disciple. You don't do that in business meetings; you just get down to business. The same applies to your company training department for things they offer employees.

Let me stop there just for a moment. I don't want to give the impression that discipling is like a business transaction. There *are* times when you need to inquire about family matters. Just this week, I learned that there was some struggle in a new marriage. We agreed that in our next meeting we would focus on that. Disciple-making is not just about checking to see what someone is getting from the Word.

Disciple-making is an art. Finding the right mix of relationship-building and disciple-making takes time. It can even vary among the men you will meet with. We all know that guy who wants to get right down to business. Then there's the other guy who needs to talk about life - a lot!

But the thing that it takes the most time is being prepared and intentional. No one walks into a business meeting without some level of preparation. There's usually an agenda; what you intend to discuss.

Let's stay at the business meeting model for just a minute longer. Many business leaders send out material to review before the meeting – beyond the agenda. This is also something that you can do as you disciple someone. Maybe you want to help a man develop a devotional time. You might send a small pdf file by email and ask him to read it before your next meeting. Obviously, you want to give him adequate time—at least a few days. Sending something ahead of time jump-starts the conversation.

I want to be careful that we do not turn disciple-making into a business transaction. However, there are things that we already do that we can bring from our work-world that can help us make disciples. And by doing that, we also give our disciples a pattern that they can repeat with someone else. After all, he now has a couple pdfs (or booklets, podcasts, books) that he can share with someone else! Then we're well on our way to making disciples who make disciples.

CHAPTER 17

What is the Great Commission?

Depending on your network, you know the answer to this, or it's actually *your* question. You've got a fifty-fifty chance of being in either of those two categories. Here's something that may shock you. The Barna Research Group found that 51 percent of churchgoers did not recognize the term "Great Commission." Another twenty-five percent knew the term but didn't know where it came from. A measly seventeen percent not only know the term but can also explain what it means![40]

Let's start from the beginning, assuming that you're in the majority group. After Jesus rose from the grave, he spent a little over a month with his disciples. During that time, Jesus talked about "next steps" with his men. That included one further command - or commission. Each Gospel writer records Jesus' command to His men a little differently. We call each of these variations "the Great Commission." But the version as it is best known comes from Matthew 28:19-20. It reads:

> "Go therefore and make disciples of all the nations, baptizing them in the name of the Father and the Son and the Holy Spirit, teaching them to observe all that I commanded you; and lo, I am with you always, even to the end of the age." (NASB)

---

[40] See "51% of Churchgoers Don't Know of the Great Commission" on Barna.com. Accessed on May 31, 2019 at: https://www.barna.com/research/half-churchgoers-not-heard-great-commission/

Plain and simple, this is the Great Commission. But it's not that easy. Many Christians and the churches where they attend can identify this charge. But there is a difference of opinion of what exactly Jesus said to do.

If you've been a Christian for any length of time, you've probably seen a church sign or banner that reads "Go." There might even be a picture of the Earth or people of different nationalities. A fair number of Christians point to *go* as the key action Jesus gave us. This idea is easy to reach when we read the version in Marks' Gospel. We read there: "Go into all the world and preach the gospel to all creation" (Mark 16:15).[41]

We see the word *go* in both verses, so it's natural to think that the emphasis should be on this action word – go. Let me explain why that's not a good conclusion; without sounding your high school English teacher. All verbs indicate an action. When there are two or more verbs in a sentence, one action is the focus (called an imperative verb).[42] Most of the other verbs (called participles) might describe how to go about doing the main action.

Let's say you come to my home through the front door. You pass through the living room into the kitchen. I realize that you left the front door open, and the cool air is getting out into the heat of South Texas. I might say, "Hey, go and close the door." There are two verbs in that sentence, but only one imperative.

You need to *go* to close the door but going isn't the key action that I'm looking for. I want the door closed. The word *close* here is the imperative verb. That's what I'm wanting you to do. You simply need to *go* to *close* the door. In this case, the word *go* is called a participle verb. (Oh, now I do sound like my high school English teacher!)

In the same way, the word *go* in Matthew's version is not the imperative verb. Jesus isn't telling them to go. Our English Bibles can mask the full tense and mood of a word. The Greek word *go* in both Matthew and Mark is in a passive nominative tense. So, many Greek scholars think that that one little word is best interpreted as "as you are going wherever it is that you go."

---

[41] Your Bible may have a note that this final portion of Mark chapter 16 is not present in many of the oldest manuscript copies that we have. That portion may have been added by a well-meaning copyist to "improve" Mark's ending.

[42] Just like all exceptions to rules of language, there can be more than one imperative verb in a sentence.

Here's the point. If I tell you to go and close the door, and all you do is go, you haven't done what I asked. How many children have been told to go and clean their room and never actually clean while they're in there?

The same grammatical rule applies to the two other participle verbs found in the sentence: *baptize* and *teach*. All three of these participles (go, baptize, and teach) are something we do, and they help us obey the Great Commission. But they aren't the main focus.

I know a few biblical Greek scholars and have read the works of many more. They all agree that the imperative verb in the Great Commission is "make disciples." It's one of those Greek words that put two words together. In English, you can translate it literally as "disciple-make." This is the action that is being commanded. The directive, the order, the charge, the mandate – the commission!

The order[43] Jesus gave His disciples at the end of his time on Earth was to make disciples. You can even say that he commissioned them to do that. If we get sidetracked with the going, baptizing, or teaching, we can be very active but not do what Jesus told us to do.[44]

So, okay. The focus is on making disciples. But why is this verse called the *Great* Commission? Why not the *Final* Commission?

No one knows when we started calling it the *Great* Commission. Most of my research points to an English missionary by the name of J. Hudson Taylor. Taylor mentioned the Great Commission often. The people who heard him or read his writings seemed to understand what he meant. He died in China in 1905, so the specific term has been around for over 100 years.

So, let me take a stab at why it is *great*. When Jesus gave this command to His disciples, the church only existed in Jerusalem. He gathered these men together and pointed them to all nations or all peoples. What a great vision. That there would be disciples of Jesus in every people group across the globe. It's not only great, but it's also intimidating, even overwhelming!

Here is what is most overwhelming, at least to me. You and I get to contribute to fulfilling this Great Commission of Jesus. Let's not get

---

[43] We usually think of judges and military officers as giving orders. But the New American Standard Version uses the word "order" coming from Jesus to his disciples in Acts 1:2!

[44] There are some mission groups that recruit young adults for one year to serve in up to eleven different countries. They are definitely going, but probably not making disciples.

lost in words, or even in the massive scope. Let's get going at being part of seeing disciples in every people group. And we start from right where we are to the very ends of the Earth (Acts 1:8)!

CHAPTER 18

What Are the Commands of Christ?

It makes sense that this question should follow the one about the Great Commission. The Great Commission in Matthew includes teaching people. It specifies that we teach them to obey everything that Christ commanded. For people to obey all this, they need to know all the commands of Jesus. So, as disciple-makers, we need to know what those commands are.

I would point out that there is a specific thought that we might not see at first glance. Jesus told His disciples this next set of disciples should be taught "to observe all that I commanded *you*." To make it clear, Jesus did not say to teach people everything that He commanded everyone. He said to teach the commands that He gave to the disciples.

Part of making disciples is teaching the commands of Jesus. And helping them obey those commands. We need to make sure that the commands apply to everyone. Jesus commanded Lazarus to come out of the grave. But that was said to Lazarus, not the disciples. He also commanded the people around Lazarus to unbind him from his grave clothes. While that was a command, it applied only in a specific situation to a specific person.

I don't intend to give you a list of commands here. If you were fully discipled, you should already know those. It won't surprise me if you don't know them, though. Barna didn't seem to ask that question in his survey on the Great Commission.[45] But I've asked some pastors and have often gotten only two or three specific commands mentioned by some.

I would suggest that you do your own Bible study. That's what I did! I took the time to read through all the words of Jesus in the four Gospels. It didn't take that much time because many Bibles put the words of Jesus in red letters! With notebook in hand, I wrote down the verses that I felt were commands that apply today. While you can find lists on the Internet of the Seven Commands or Forty-Nine Commands, I came up with about ten clear commands.

I will give you three commands to get you started. The Great Commission in Matthew 28:19-20 would be the first one. The Great Commandment is found in Matthew 22:37-38. And the New Commandment is in John 13:34-35. Everyone should agree on at least these three.

You should look for the other commands of Christ as you read the Gospels. Find those that Jesus gave to people, not to one specific person. These are often repeated, perhaps with slightly different words, in more than one Gospel. (The New Commandment is an exception as it was only recorded by John.) While the command given to a paralyzed man to pick up his sleeping mat and walk is in three Gospels (Matthew, Mark, and Luke). But that command only applied to that man, not to all of us.

Now, once you've found the commands of Christ, there's one more thing that you need to do. We need to have a way to teach someone how to obey each command. That just might be easier said than done. Let's look at one of the three commands I just listed above to decide how we can teach an emerging disciple* how to obey that one.

Let's look at the New Commandment from the Gospel of John, where Jesus said:

> "A new command I give you: Love one another. As I have loved you, so you must love one another. By this everyone will know that you are my disciples, if you love one another."

Sometimes we may need to decide if this command was given to all of Jesus' disciples. This one is clear-cut. It was directed to the

---

[45] See "51% of Churchgoers Don't Know of the Great Commission" on Barna.com. Accessed on May 31, 2019 at: https://www.barna.com/research/half-churchgoers-not-heard-great-commission/

disciples who were gathered together on the night Jesus would be arrested.

You want to show your emerging disciple what action is supposed to be taken. Jesus says, "Love one another." He also clarified this as loving each other in the same way that he loved them. He said this immediately after washing their feet before supper (see John 13:5).

The hardest part of obeying a command is making it practical and achievable to the emerging disciple. We all think we know what it means to love someone else. But most people feel loved not by the way that we feel, but by an action toward them motivated by our feelings. We may feel that we've acted lovingly, but the real judge of love is the other person.

We want the emerging disciple to have a way to measure how well he's doing at obeying this command. Jesus said that people will be able to identify a disciple be the way he loves others. In this case, it's not the person loving, or the person being loved who determines the action. It's "everyone" (NIV) or "all men" (NASB). We might want to check the box ourselves, but Jesus puts the pen in someone else's hand.

Each command we teach to an emerging disciple needs to be clear. It needs to be something that applies to him. We need to talk about how we will go about obeying the command. And we need a way of measuring success.

You can expect that some commands will be harder to follow than others. I had a roommate who would yell at his mother over the phone. (She lived in another state.) I talked with him about the fourth commandment (of the Old Testament Ten Commandments). I explained how Jesus talked about the importance of obeying this very command (Mark 7:9-13).

As we talked about it, his first reaction was to mention how difficult his mother was. I asked him if the command had an exception clause – it didn't. So, we began to work on the way to honor his mother the way Jesus expected. It was hard, but he soon began to experience success. And that changed the entire relationship between him and his mother.

We can't only teach the commands of Jesus from an informational stance. We need to help our emerging disciples figure out how to make the necessary changes in their lives that are rooted in those commands. We can celebrate each small victory and keep at it until we get a pattern of obedience in each of the commands of Jesus.

This is also why meeting one-on-one is so helpful. We can teach commands from the pulpit and in small groups. But working out the details in a person's life usually means being up close and personal.

Who Was the Great Commission Intended For?

First, let's look at a specific recording of the Great Commission. Most people will point to Matthew 28:19-20 for the Great Commission. Some others, though—and they are correct—point to a few other verses that also record a version of the Great Commission.

Matthew records his version of the Great Commission in this way:

> And Jesus came up and spoke to them, saying, "All authority has been given to Me in heaven and on Earth. Go therefore and make disciples of all the nations, baptizing them in the name of the Father and the Son and the Holy Spirit, teaching them to observe all that I commanded you; and lo, I am with you always, even to the end of the age." (NASB)

That begins with verse eighteen. Some people leave that verse out, but it shows the divine authority upon which Jesus can command us.

I mentioned other verses that support the Great Commission. These may have slightly different points of focus, but they still tell us what we should be doing. They include Mark 16:14–18, Luke 24:44–49, John 20:19–23, and Acts 1:4-8.

From a theology standpoint, I do need to address one of those passages. Most of the oldest copies of existing manuscripts the Gospel of Mark do not contain the verses beyond verse eight in the last chapter. If you look in your Bible, you're likely to see verses 9 through

20 in brackets. Your Bible may also add a note that these verses were missing from the earliest manuscripts.

Many Bible experts believe that a scribe added "the end of the story." It seems that this began to appear in second-century copies of Mark. A different third-century copy only adds verse 20 after verse eight. There are over 1,200 existing copies that do contain Mark 16:9-20. We simply don't know if the young man, who was discipled by Barnabas, Paul, and Peter, named John Mark wrote those words.

It seems most likely that this part of Mark was not in the original Gospel. We still have four other passages that record how Jesus sent his Apostles out to the world with His message. When we compare the Mark version to the others, we can see that there's no major conflict—or you might say, "Nothing lost, nothing gained." Because of the four passages, we can be sure that Jesus wanted his message spread.

Now back to our question. Does this commission apply to us today? In most evangelical churches, we will hear that we need to contribute, in some way, to the Great Commission. It hasn't always been that way. Ruth Tucker, who studies the history of missions, pointed out that during the Reformation, Martin Luther thought this commission was only for the twelve Apostles.[46] On the other hand, Luther's contemporary, John Calvin, sent four missionaries to Brazil in 1551, but later Calvinists did not take up the commission.[47] Or maybe we could say they set it aside.

Things can get more complicated. We may tend to "pick" a commission that best suits our fancy. That can result in differences in *how* the Great Commission is accomplished. For example, a college campus ministry that I support financially takes its mission statement from Mark 16. Their emphasis is to "preach the gospel to all creation" (from Mark 16:15), without much emphasis on disciple-making. Another group uses Luke 24:47 to understand that preaching repentance is the focus. Another group uses John 20:22 to offer forgiveness to all.

Only Matthew uses the word "disciple" in his rendition of the Great Commission. No other Great Commission verse contains this

---

[46] Ruth A. Tucker, *From Jerusalem to Irian Jaya: A Biographical History of Christian Missions*. Second Edition. (Grand Rapids: Zondervan Publishing House, 2004), 97.

[47] Kenneth B. Mulholland, "From Luther to Carey: Pietism and the Modern Missionary Movement" in *Bibliotheca Sacra*, 156:621 (Jan 1999), 85.

expected outcome. The other verses focus on what those who were being commissioned were to do. Matthew has those "do" portions but also provides the final objective.

And it's in the final outcome that we find our answer to whether this still applies to us today. Let's look closely at it, found in the first half of verse 20:

"teaching them to observe all that I commanded you."

I think we can all agree the first Apostles made disciples. As they shared the gospel, which included repentance and forgiveness (Acts 2:38, 3:19, and 5:31), they baptized and taught. They taught them all the commands Jesus had given. And they taught in a way to produce obedience.

The Great Commission is actually a command. The Greek word that we translate to "make disciples" is an imperative – a command. And as a command, it would be the last command Jesus gave to His disciples. If those disciples were to obey the Great Commission, it had to include teaching others to obey even the last command – to make disciples.

The process of making a disciple will not be complete until the new disciple knows how to make disciples himself. But, not only to know how to make a disciple but to actually do that himself. This second-generation disciple would now know and obey all of Jesus' commands, including the command to make disciples.

That might sound confusing, so let me put some identifiers on them. The Apostles are group A. They begin to make disciples who are baptized and taught to obey (group B). Now group B begins to make disciples – a group C is born. Group C leads to group D, and so on.

Here's what that means. Group D above now has learned the commands of Christ and seeks to obey them. That includes the last command of Christ – to make disciples. They will make disciples of group E in a never-ending process of spiritual reproduction. Each new generation of believers becomes responsible for making disciples in the next generation.

Someone helped you become a Christian. It might be that they simply shared the gospel and set you in a nursery for someone else to care for. But as you grow as a disciple, you must come to grips with the last command of Jesus – to make disciples who will make more disciples.

The command, the Great Commission, applies to us today, just as it did to the Apostles in the first century.

Why Don't People Make Disciples?

Let me give you the full question as it was posed to me. "Why don't people disciple? Or, what is getting in the way? Do you think it's more a genuine lack of training or commitment to the call?" A pretty long question – more like three-in-one, maybe even four-in-one. The first question identified the problem. The other questions look for a reason why. You could also say that there's an assumption built into the first question – that people don't make disciples.

Let me go to that assumption first and validate it. It is a fact; people don't make disciples. Disciple-makers make disciples. And to be a disciple-maker you first need to be a disciple. So, we find an assumption within the assumption. That is, people don't make disciples because they aren't disciples. Because only disciples can make a disciple.

The idea that *people* can make disciples implies that *anyone* in any church setting can do it. For some reason, they just don't. It's the idea that's the wrong conclusion. Here's why. We can't even be sure that everyone in a church is a believer in Jesus. The growth of seeker-sensitive churches should help us see that. A church may attract a non-Christian through its programs. But until that person comes to Christ, we surely can't expect him to make a disciple.

Even when he becomes a believer, he's not ready to make disciples himself. He needs to grow in his walk with Christ before he can help someone else do the same. Now, that's not to say that he needs to be completely mature to disciple another person. He only needs to be a few steps ahead of the other guy. But he needs to be taking some steps; to actively be making some progress.

Many churches are making progress at getting new Christians into some type of follow-up. Helping them develop their walk with Christ. A walk centered around a life of faith at home and work rather than just inside the church walls. Other churches seem to focus more on getting a new Christian to help with parking or welcome others at the door. Great serving activities, but by themselves, they don't help someone become a disciple.

I'm moving toward the "what gets in the way" question. And in some cases, it's the church that gets in the way. Sometimes, we're asking the new Christian to serve at a church when we should be serving the new Christian. But we can't point a finger that the church without several other fingers pointing back at us!

Like it or not, as adults, we're responsible for our own growth. Someday, Jesus may ask some of us why we didn't become a disciple or make some ourselves. The church building won't be there to point at. We also won't be able to point to our parents, living conditions, or any other variable. Here's part of my own story related to that.

I became a Christian in April 1974. I became part of a group of disciples. Right up to September of 1975. That month, I moved from Fort Knox to Gelnhausen, Germany. I went to a post with 2,000 other soldiers. After a month of searching, I realized that I was one of three known Christians. The other two were a chaplain and a missionary wife who played the organ. There might have been some incognito Christians, but I couldn't flush them out.

I knew that if I did not fight for my Christian walk, there would be consequences. I knew the basics*, and I determined that I would practice them diligently. By myself. At least until some other Christians closer to my age arrived.

It was a time before the Internet. I wrote back to America to get books and tapes that would help me grow stronger in the basics. A letter took a week to arrive. A package took up to a month. But I didn't let these speedbumps hinder me. They might have slowed me down, but I was still going to make progress.

I lived that way for two years. Finally, another Christian showed up. But only because I led him to Christ. Now I had someone to disciple, as well as a spiritual battle buddy. It was another six months before another Christian arrived to join in fellowship with us.

When I came to Germany, I had a grasp of the basics, but over time got a strong grip on them. Without any distractions, I could focus on time in the Word and prayer. My training came from books and cassette tapes (I still have many of those). Getting that kind of training took a deep commitment.

I've now entered into the training versus commitment part of this question. In almost every way, this training comes from outside of ourselves. Someone begins to provide a young Christian the training to be a disciple and then to make disciples. That comes by either being in front of us or through a media source. We may need to position ourselves in the right place. But we simply can't get away with saying we have no access today.

Commitment comes from inside of ourselves. Business leaders will tell you that motivation comes from within a person. The leader can't motivate others. He can provide an environment, but people need to develop motivation themselves.[48]

We have access to training in the spiritual basics through people or media sources. We also have access to Scripture at our fingertips. The Bible is right on your smartphone now. And the Bible gives us everything we need to find the commitment to grow as disciples who make disciples.

And there's the most basic, underlying problem. The real answer to this honest question. We don't *not* make disciples because we aren't disciples. We don't *not* have the training available nor the commitment that it takes. Instead, it's because we aren't in the Bible ourselves to see what it plainly says.

My time in Germany proved this point to me. *No* distraction did then, or will now, keep me from being a disciple who makes disciples. I'm only distracted when my motivation wanes. My motivation wanes when I'm not abiding in God's Word. In other words, *I* am the one who keeps me from being a disciple who makes disciples.

---

[48] See "If You Want to Motivate Someone, Do This" by Laura Garnett. Accessed on July 19, 2019 at: https://www.inc.com/laura-garnett/if-you-want-to-motivate-someone-do-this.html

How Did Jesus Make Disciples?

There are several books of various lengths available that explore this question. I would highly recommend *The Training of the Twelve* by A. B. Bruce, which is a longer read. Here, I have no intention of giving a long answer, but a simple overview of what Jesus did.

Before I answer further, I'd like to give you some cautions. What Jesus did was in a very specific context. I am sure that you're in a different context. Jesus spent most of his time in Galilee, though he did travel into Judah and some surrounding Gentile regions. My point is that his context included highly religious people who had some real hopes. We shouldn't expect the same kind of response from a different context, and many of us are in a very different postmodern context.

Jesus also spent at least one night in prayer before he invited men to follow him. It could be that he spent several more days and capped it off with a night of prayer. (I like to look to see what the Bible says, and what the Bible *doesn't* say. But I want to avoid speculation at the same time.) My point is that while Jesus covered his call to men with prayer, we may tend to do less of that.

There are also some assumptions that we may make about the beginning of Jesus' ministry. The Gospels seem to open with his invitation to follow him. That doesn't mean the earliest disciples didn't know him until he randomly walked up and told them to leave their nets.

It's just possible that Jesus had been down in the area of Capernaum for a while. Some Bible scholars believe that he even had moved into his own house there. If that's the case, people already knew him. We have no way of knowing that this was true. We also don't have a way of knowing that it was false.

So, as we begin to explore this answer, let's keep in mind *our* context, prayer, and exposure. These will affect how you try to implement discipling the way Jesus did. And I've got to say that he was a great model!

Several Bible teachers point out that Jesus didn't have a classroom. (I can just imagine sitting in a Bible classroom and hearing a teacher say that!) The norm was for a local rabbi to gather some young men together into a synagogue room and teach. Instead, Jesus had more of an apprentice-style of discipling. Even though he was often called "Rabbi," Jesus didn't seem to follow the norm.

Jesus did seem first to offer men a glimpse of his life. The Gospel of John starts with Jesus saying, "Come and see," when asked where he lived (John 1:38). Only a few verses later, he invites Philip to "Come with me" (John 1:43).

Here's something handy for you to pick up from this part of the story. The first two guys who asked Jesus where he stayed, did so based on a remark from John the Baptist (John 1:36-37). Peter gets involved when Andrew, one of the first two men who heard John's remark, tells him about Jesus. The next day, Jesus invites Philip, who is from the same town as Andrew and Peter (John 1:44). Then Philip seeks out Nathaniel and says, "Come and see!" These were not random men. They were connected as family and neighbors all from the same town.

Now, I'm not saying that you should look to your family and neighbors to make a disciple. I'm pointing out that Jesus wasn't working in a vacuum. Too often we gloss over these details and make bad assumptions. That can set us up for failure—even when we think we're just doing what Jesus did.

It appears these first four disciples were asked to "come" by Jesus over three days. Then, two days later, they're all together at a wedding in Cana. Wait; there's another detail. All four of these first men were from Bethsaida. That's on the north end of the Sea (Lake) of Galilee, where the Jordan River flows into the lake. Two days later, they're in Cana (John 2:1). Cana is close to Nazareth, in the heart of Galilee. It's about 20 miles from Bethsaida; most of it uphill. It probably took a full day just to walk to Cana!

Here's my point. Jesus takes these guys on a road trip (backpacking?) while still in the "come and see" phase of discipling. There are some very calculated things happening in these first five days. And here's my point. We often think about being intentional when making disciples (and so we should). How intentional are we at *choosing* disciples? If we don't get this part down, we shouldn't expect to see results like what Jesus had.

Side note: All my old Navigator mentors taught the "principle" of a road trip. Skip would say, "Never go on a drive without someone else in tow." Road trips are by far some of the best discipling times we can ever encounter. We can definitely experience a man as he really is, and he can see the same in us!

After the Cana wedding, which may have covered up to a week, Jesus and his four disciples head back to Capernaum. This time he has his mother and brothers along with him (John 2:12). At least the walk back was mostly downhill, but it probably took another full day of walking with this larger group.

After being there for a few days, Jesus and his disciples head to Jerusalem for Passover. They really get to see him in action there. Driving out sheep from the temple. Turning over tables. Getting into a conflict with the leading Jews. These disciples later remember that the Old Testament Scripture said, "My love for your house is like a fire burning in me" (John 2:17, Worldwide English New Testament). That doesn't mean they made a connection beyond Jesus being hot-blooded. But they're being exposed to him day-by-day.

By the time we get to John chapter six, we have a second Passover. A year has passed. Philip, Andrew, and Peter, three of the first four disciples, are mentioned here. We will need to move to another Gospel. Matthew will tell us how Jesus added to his disciples and began to change his methods.

Matthew 4:21 will add James and John to the group. The end of the chapter has Jesus as he is teaching, proclaiming the good news, and healing the sick. We can assume that at least six of the disciples are with him at this point. Perhaps more since large crowds are beginning to follow him (Matthew 4:25).

After the Sermon on the Mount (Matthew 5-7) and more healing, Matthew is called to follow Jesus (Matthew 9:9). While Matthew uses the term "follow me," instead of "come and see," the results would have been the same. Matthew even records the importance of following as more critical than family (Matthew 8:18-22).

By the time we reach the end of Matthew 9, Jesus continues to teach, proclaim, and heal. With compassion for the crowds around him, he tells the disciples to pray for harvest workers (Matthew 9:38). Then, Jesus chooses the twelve men in whom he will invest his life (Matthew 10:1). And with some general guidelines, he sends them on their first short-term mission trip (Matthew 10:5-15).

Matthew doesn't give us details of the trip, but Mark's Gospel does. They went out and did the same things that Jesus had been doing; that teaching, proclaiming, and healing part, along with casting out demons (Mark 6:12-13, 30). They had seen Jesus do all these things. The following and seeing had an impact on them and those they reached.

Once the twelve disciples returned, they told Jesus their stories (Mark 6:30). The next verse has Jesus saying, "Let's get some alone time" (that's the Bruce version). I don't think that Jesus interrupted their stories. I would imagine that he listened to all the details. Once that was done, he got some downtime – at least while on the boat (Mark 6:32).

There's a principle here. The people that you are discipling have stories to tell. Part of discipling is letting those stories come out. These are choice times when we can encourage them in what they're doing and feeling.

Just yesterday (from when I write this portion), I met with a 25-year-old "live wire." I had prepared some great content to share with him. I had a bookmark in my Bible and was all prayed up. But when we got to the coffee shop, there was just something in his face. I mentally set aside my plan and let him talk. At the end of our meeting, I not only got a hug. He thanked me for listening.

Don't lose this listening time between verses 30 and 31 of Mark 6. It's another one of those areas that we might gloss over. We can't read into the text that Jesus wasn't interested in their stories. Discipling includes listening!

Luke is going to pick up Jesus' discipling method in chapter ten. Now Jesus is sending out 72 disciples. Strategically, he seems to be telling them to go to specific towns. It seems that he intends to go there, so he has them become "little Elijahs" to prepare the way. They've got guidelines that are like those from the first mission trip.

This idea of watching first, then doing seems to be the basic way that Jesus equipped his disciples. It culminates in the Great Commission which points to all nations (every people group) as the ultimate target. We, like those original disciples, are to reach the nations by making disciples who make more disciples.

CHAPTER 22

Is Everyone Called to Make Disciples?

This question is like the one about the Great Commission. There is a difference, though. Someone can believe the Great Commission is active and applies to the Church today. Yet, for some reason, that same person may feel that they should not make disciples. The question is further complicated by using the term "called."

The thinking behind this question could be about personal gifting, maturity, or readiness. If so, this question could easily be included in Part One on being a disciple. Yet, I think it belongs here better.

Let's address the term "called" first. Does anyone need to be called to obey a command? Is making disciples a calling? If it *is* a calling, then only those who are called should do so. That last statement allows someone who doesn't feel called to exclude this from their Christian lives. Don't trust those feelings!

The term "called" is used very broadly, not only in the church but even in the secular world now. Vocational counselors in high schools and colleges talk about being called to certain types of work. There is no biblical meaning to the word when used this way.

In the Bible, the word *called* can imply being called out from something (1 Peter 2:9). Christians are called out of the world, into the church. Ministry leaders are called out of the congregation, into leadership. The word *called* simply doesn't fit when it comes to making disciples. If you have been called out of the world and into the Christian life, that calling included to make disciples. They go hand in hand together.

Jesus commanded us to make disciples. He also commanded us to love one another. And He commanded us to be witnesses. None of these things are dependent on a calling. They each apply to anyone who responded to the call to come to Christ in faith. We surely would never say that we're not called to love someone. We wouldn't tell a judge and jury that we weren't called to be a witness – although they do call a witness to the stand. Responding to a call to witness in a court trial is part of being a citizen of legal standing.

Every Christian is called to make disciples. But not everyone is mature or ready.

Think of it this way. Most people have a desire to be married and have a family. But even if they feel ready to marry, they must be of legal age to do that. You simply can't get a marriage license when you're fourteen years old (no matter how much you've fallen in love). You're not mature enough.

I often talk with guys about marriage. One of my favorite questions is: "Are you ready to be married?" I often hear, "Not quite yet." Maybe they want to finish college. Or get out of debt. Or live on their own for a year. There's a readiness involved in marriage. The wise man waits until he's ready. But he also is doing something to get ready! And if you're not ready to make disciples, you should do something to get ready—get equipped (Ephesians 4:12).

Gifting doesn't apply to getting married unless you consider being single a gift (1 Corinthians 7:7). And gifting doesn't apply to disciple-making. Gifting can, although, influence your style of disciple-making.

How many times have I heard someone say, "I don't have the gift of evangelism"? Evangelism may be a gift, but every disciple of Jesus was commanded to be his witness (Acts 1:8). Some may be gifted and do it better, but all of us need to be ready to witness. There simply is no spiritual gift of disciple-making. Certain gifts may help someone make disciples more quickly, more often, or more deeply.

There might be a factor of maturity. A three-year-old child cannot reproduce, even though they may like to play house. They simply aren't physically mature enough to have children themselves. But the timeline for maturity in Christ does not take 15 to 20 years to begin to reproduce. If properly trained, people can lead others to Christ and begin to disciple them. There aren't many people in their first year as a believer who share their faith and see someone come to Christ. Yet, I led someone to Christ just 361 days after I became a Christian myself and started to disciple him.

If you feel that you're not mature enough, get discipled! Spending time with a trusted disciple-maker can help you be ready in six months or less. No Master of Divinity is necessary!

CHAPTER 23

Can I Be a Disciple-Maker?

I believe this question arises from one of two concerns. You either feel unqualified or disqualified. You either feel that you don't know enough, or you're too young in the faith, making you unqualified. Or you had a major struggle with a sinful habit; maybe you still do. And you feel that with that history you have been taken out of the game.

Truthfully, to disciple someone, you only need to be a few steps ahead of him. Literally, just a few. When I came to Christ, it was a bank teller who began to help me grow in my faith. One of the things he asked me to do was memorize five Bible verses: one verse a week for a month. I did okay the first two weeks; maybe it was due to the excitement of having a new life.

But the third week the verse I was asked to memorize was longer. I struggled to get started just because it seemed to cover the entire little card it was printed on. After a week, I was asked if I had learned the verse. I couldn't even cite the reference, much less the words of the verse.

The next week I could only cite the reference and give a general idea of what the verse was about. The third week my disciple-maker didn't even ask if I had finished the verse. He seemed to assume that I wasn't going to get it done. I felt awful; like I had disappointed him.

So that week, I worked hard to memorize that third verse (it happened to be I Corinthians 10:13). Once I learned the verse, I realized how helpful it was to me. So, I set myself to memorize the other two verses to catch up to where I was "supposed" to be. Then someone else told me about a packet of eight more verses, and I memorized the first two of those. I was on a roll!

When it came time to meet with my disciple-maker, I asked him if he would quiz me on that third verse. He seemed surprised that I had finally gotten it done. I quoted it perfectly! And he was very encouraged by my work. Then I began to quote the next four verses that I had memorized that week. His look of pleasure seemed to turn to a look of shock. But he was still quite encouraging.

About a year later, I was talking to the man who had been mentoring my disciple-maker. He laughed as he told me how my disciple-maker talked with him about my memorizing five verses in one week. He wasn't concerned about my pace; he was concerned about his own. He had thought if he stayed two verses ahead of me, he was fine. He slowed down when I slowed down. But when I learned five verses in one week (without warning him), I had jumped two verses ahead of him!

The fact that I knew more verses than my disciple-maker (only for a season) didn't make him any less of a disciple-maker. He was still helping me in other areas that I needed a lot of help in. And my own progress actually served to push him to be more diligent in his own disciplines, including in Scripture memory.

In fact, I have often encouraged someone who feels unqualified to begin to disciple another man. I find that there's a self-motivating pressure to grow stronger when you're helping another guy.

Here's another story from my past. About a year after I became a Christian, I spent the night at my "spiritual" grandfather's house (his name was Cecil). That was the man who was helping my disciple-maker. Another fellow also spent the night, both of us in sleeping bags in the basement. He saw me the next morning reading my Bible and began to ask questions. His questions resulted in me sharing the gospel and leading my first man to Christ.

I was really excited and went upstairs to tell the rest of the house what had just happened. Not considering that it was only 6:00 A.M., I knocked on Cecil's bedroom door. He came to the door mumbling about the early Saturday morning arousal.

I quickly told him that the fellow downstairs had just come to Christ. And I pressed him that he should go downstairs to begin the follow-up* process for this new believer. He looked at me through sleepy eyes and said, "That's your baby. You change his diapers." I was horrified! He wanted *me* to take responsibility for a new believer. Really?

I said I didn't know what to do, and I'd only been a Christian for a year (actually, four days short of a year). Cecil asked me if I remembered how my disciple-maker taught me how to read the Bible and pray. Of course, I remembered that. He told me to start there. If I got stuck, he was willing to help me. But I needed to help my new believer by myself. And he did help me when I got stuck.

Here's why that was important. Several months later, the Army sent me to central Germany. When I arrived, I found that I was the only Christian serviceman around my age. But I was able to feed myself spiritually and pray effectively. I had also learned how to share the gospel and follow-up on new believers. As a few more guys came to Christ from my witness, I was able to help them grow in these same areas. Without any other help than prayers on the other side of the Atlantic Ocean. All because Cecil pushed me to disciple a man myself.

Maybe you don't feel fully qualified to disciple someone. If that's the case, find someone to help you while you start to help someone else. It might take you a little time to find your helper. But in the meantime, help the guy who's right in front of you. (If you can't find help, join the *Disciple-Making Questions* group on Facebook.)

Now on to the more sensitive issue of feeling disqualified. Even the Apostle Paul had a concern about not being qualified (1 Corinthians 9:27). Now to be clear, he wasn't implying that he had done something that disqualified him. Instead, he was doing things to stay qualified. But when you feel disqualified, it's tough to invest in someone else.

Perhaps you find that you didn't do things like Paul to stay in the race, to compete in the game (1 Corinthians 9:24-25). You feel, perhaps rightly, that something you have done or didn't do prevents you from making disciples. I would challenge that thought.[49]

Is this thing you struggled with is in the past? Then you need to remind yourself that God's grace and mercy have been applied. All sin is forgiven through the blood of Jesus Christ. Now it does have its consequences even with forgiveness. However, the command of Jesus to make disciples still applies, even to you.

------

[49] There are consequences to our sin. However, we may apply heavy consequences ourselves, rather than let God apply consequences to his standard. Jerry Bridges' book *Transforming Grace* may be helpful for you if you're struggling with this.

Is this thing you struggle with is in the present? Then you need to do something about it before starting to help another person. Get help yourself. You can choose an accountability relationship, a community group, or pastoral or professional counseling. Just take the steps needed to improve your condition. Please!

I know men who have struggled with same-sex attraction. Yet when they get the help they need, they *can* disciple others. I know men who have been separated or divorced. Yet when they get help, they *can* disciple others. In many cases, they can disciple men similar to themselves. And they can do that even better than those who have not had the same trouble.

Your church may have standards for leadership that you don't meet. I know some churches that do not allow a divorced man to be an elder or pastor. But that's not we're aiming for. Ephesians 4:11-12 lets us that leaders of the church are given by God to equip that saints for ministry. That's *you* being equipped for ministry. Broken, messed up you.

We can see several men in the Old Testament who messed up pretty bad. Moses was a murderer. So was King David; he murdered to hide his adultery. You're not all that bad! We *all* have our baggage.

So, whether you feel unqualified or disqualified, I strongly encourage you to do what it takes to get into the race. It's a long race, but you can do it!

CHAPTER 24

Can I Disciple My Children?

This will probably be the most controversial answer that I give. I recently was having breakfast with a friend in Bowling Green, Kentucky. When this subject came up, I told him my conclusion. I was quickly told that he would "instruct me in the way more perfectly" (Acts 18:26). His instruction backfired, and my response hasn't changed.

There are many opinions that will conflict with part or all of my answer. Just the past Sunday (as I wrote this), my pastor was speaking about church leaders needing to keep their children disciplined. On the screen, he showed the two words disciple and discipline and explained that they come from the same root word.

That's true. In English, they do come from the same root word. But not in the original common Greek that the New Testament was written in. The word for disciple in Greek is *mathētēs*. The Greek words for discipline are either *paideia* or *sōphronismos*. You can easily look at these words and see there is no common root between them.

I often talk with married men about finding someone to disciple. Many of them say that they are discipling their children. I get it. Most married men are busy with work and family life and squeeze in church. Yet, this reply is often an excuse for not discipling another adult male. That's pretty much taking the easy way out of our responsibility to the Great Commission. Ouch!

Later in this book, I will talk about how long it takes to disciple someone. Let's face it, most men have at least eighteen years to "disciple" their children. And much of that discipling time is in the evening or on the weekends. Using the kids as a reason for not taking an hour or two out of your week is... well, you finish the sentence!

But back to the point. Can you disciple your children? Yes. (That's a weak yes.) Can you disciple a ten-year-old (or younger)? No. And this answer is based on the traits of a disciple as laid out by Jesus (see Section One on *Being a Disciple*, especially chapter eight). My answer is not based on the local church's use of "discipleship," which would include Sunday School, AWANAs or Trail Life, and even Vacation Bible School.

Here's why I say that. Earlier in Section One, we looked at six key verses quoting Jesus. Let's just take the very first one we find in Luke's gospel:

> "If anyone comes to me and does not hate father and mother, wife and children, brothers and sisters—yes, even their own life—such a person cannot be my disciple" (Luke 14:26).

Here is a clear qualification for being a disciple right from the lips of Jesus. We've all heard a sermon on how the word "hate" is comparative. Compared to how much you love Jesus, it looks like you hate your parents. You actively decide to follow Jesus over and above your parents, or siblings, or children, and even your wife.

I know adults who have difficulty with this verse. They haven't yet heard the sermon that explains the comparative "hate." It takes some time to process what that looks like in their own life. Once they understand it, they can decide if they're willing to do that. And it *is* a decision. It doesn't just happen.

So, if we're honest, this kind of comparative feeling is very difficult for a child to understand, much less decide to employ. Children simply aren't mature enough, either emotionally or intellectually, to do this. Sure, they can be moving in that direction; with our help. But they're not there yet. And Jesus said unless you can do it, you aren't his disciple. That pretty much excludes most children.

And I don't think there's a specific age when a child is ready to become a disciple. One of my spiritual sons has four children. Of the three boys, the two younger ones are beginning to ask questions about faith and baptism. The oldest boy isn't interested in any of that.

I suspect that part of the reason for this is that the oldest boy is more like his mom. Dad is trying to take the lead here, but their relationship doesn't gel the same as the younger boys. Dad may need to step aside and let mom develop the boy during this phase of life.

Yet, there comes a time when neither parent can give input, much less disciple. We all know how teenagers think that a parent knows less than a rock. While that seems to go away around the age of 25, it's painful for the parents. Especially parents that are trying to raise up young disciples. So, they may need to be willing to let someone else take the primary role of disciple-maker. But you're really not discipling; *you're* parenting—laying a foundation that others will later build on.

I recently had a nineteen-year-old move into my home. His Christian home was rigid. He was homeschooled and went to a very conservative church. As a college student, he was trying to become an independent adult. Mom, in her efforts to "raise up a child in the way he should go," kept laying down more rules. He responded by rebelling.

Part of his rebellion was to find a place of his own. That happened to be my place. He told his mother some of the benefits of living with me. It was a home with three other Christians. Another reason was that I would mentor him. His mother replied, "I can mentor you!" (Millennials and Gen Z often use the term "mentor" as a substitute for "disciple.") However, we understand the word mentor, I'm pretty sure most moms can't mentor their 19-year-old sons.

I went through this myself. I was frustrated that I couldn't speak into the life of one of my teenagers. I talked with the pastor about it, who had his own kids at similar ages. He said, "I don't think a father can disciple a child. Let us (a church small group) work on that for you." What a relief!

There are always exceptions to this. Of course, you will do much better than the average parent. Maybe you even did (from an ivory palace). But overall, parents really can't disciple their children. They parent them.

Part of parenting is teaching biblical and social values as a child becomes ready to learn. That parenting process will take at least eighteen years and perhaps more. It includes exposing them to the Christian faith and answering questions (which often seem to come up during bath time). It's ensuring that they are involved in activities that support the faith. There's much we can do – including, most of all, prayer.

All these activities set up a child to grow mature in faith and someday become a disciple. But we shouldn't be shocked when they finally become a disciple somewhere outside the home. Maybe through a church youth ministry, or a college campus ministry. But we *can* set the foundation.

Lay a foundation of faith to develop in your children. Pray that they become disciples. Invest in them deeply. But don't let them be an excuse for not discipling another man who's waiting for someone to invest in him, as well.

How Do I Know Who to Disciple?

I received multiple versions of this question. It was most interesting to me that they came primarily from men who were already making disciples. Perhaps that means that men who are new to making disciples have not yet considered the question. Or maybe if a man disciples enough fellows, he begins to think about how to narrow the field.

Let's start with the most obvious answer. You can only disciple someone nearby. You simply can't (maybe the right word is shouldn't) disciple your old college buddy who now lives on the opposite side of the country. Yes, you can connect through the Internet. Just like you can find a potential spouse through a dating site. But there are better ways.

Case in point. I met a fellow (I'll call him Steve) at church who seemed to need some discipling. When we got together, he explained that he had "accountability partners" that he talked to "regularly." Me being me, I asked a few more questions. I could easily tell that he did, in fact, need some discipling. Yet, he was sure that his relationships with old college buddies would be adequate.

They weren't. Steve got into several difficulties, including an intimate relationship with a non-Christian gal. Many of his difficulties could have been discussed in a face-to-face meeting. But the monthly online meetings were more about four guys catching up on life. There was minimal accountability. And his behavior began to get out of hand.

Being around someone is an important aspect of discipling them. There's just something about looking at each other in the eye. Not that a discipling relationship is completely built around accountability, but that is part of it.

So, who is right in front of you? There are a surprising number of men in the church who have never been discipled. You'll just have to be watchful and quick. They're usually the ones who arrive at the last minute and get out during the closing song!

Many churches today have a time when you greet people around you. One day during this time, I quickly surveyed the area around me. Four rows back was a young couple who were not wearing their Sunday best. He had on walking shorts and a white t-shirt. He had tattoos that fully covered his left arm and left leg, but none on the right side. He looked completely out of place among the business-casual crowd around him.

I worked my way back to Andrew (obviously not his real name) and shook his hand. I also asked him to stay afterward so I could talk more. (Have you noticed how the music resumes just as you get into a good conversation?) And as the service ended, I turned to wave at him just in case he tried to escape! (I was 'in pursuit!")

It was another nice, short talk. He was new to the area and was looking for work. I offered to buy him lunch that week, and he agreed. Many suspicions began to come together at that first lunch. He only had tattoos on the left side because he was right-handed. He learned to tattoo while in prison – for murder.

Andrew was visited by a prison ministry worker who left him a New Testament. He had read it multiple times and prayed the prayer printed on the inside back cover. He picked the church because he saw it right off the major roadway. He wanted to grow as a Christian, stay out of prison, and be a good husband. Disciple-making material! Easy pickings! And he was right in front of me — okay, technically right behind me!

I'm convinced that when we are open to discipling men, God will place them near us. They may not always be someone we want to bring home to the family — at least not right away. But they're there. Note: Your family can benefit from meeting someone like Andrew, and Andrew will greatly benefit when he meets your family.

Now to get to the question behind this question. How do I know who to disciple — and not get burned? Why does a disciple-maker ask this kind of question? It usually means that he's had a couple bad experiences and wants to avoid any more of those.

If this is what you're really asking, here's my most simple answer: There's no magic formula. The guy who looks golden can be a complete failure. The guy who looks hopeless can be your best disciple.

Here's another story. I worked on an Army post and lived nearby. I started to disciple a young believer — he asked for help — and I'll call him Randy. He was tall, dark, and handsome with an engaging personality. As I was helping Randy develop his devotional life, we would meet at my living room on Saturday mornings. We would read a passage of Scripture and pray together. By learning to do this on Saturdays, Randy also began to do it during the week. Yea; he caught the bug!

Everything pointed to Randy growing as a disciple and doing very well at it. So well that my severely introverted wife thought the world of him. It was her idea to allow Randy to spend the weekends in the spare bedroom, instead of the Army barracks. Once a month, my wife and I would go to San

Antonio for a weekend, and we would leave Randy in charge of the house.

Now, my wife was a clean freak. Since we wouldn't get home until late on Sunday, she meticulously cleaned the house before we left. That included washing the linens, so they were nice and fresh when we fell into bed after a long weekend.

One Sunday night, I was ready to dive into bed. But my focus was interrupted by my wife calling me from the bathroom. I diverted to the bathroom to see what was wrong. She was pointing to a small trash can. It was empty when we left on Friday. And she asked if the contents were mine.

Inside the trash can was a used condom and the wrapper. (Sorry if that offends you reading about it but think about how my wife felt.) I explained that it was my brand, but she already knew that I didn't throw these in the trash.

My wife then marched into the bedroom and pulled down the covers. It was obvious that the bed had been slept in – which she had skillfully made before we left on Friday. Randy had slept in our bed, with someone else. He even went into my nightstand to take a condom. We felt completely violated.

I tried to be reasonable and rational the next day when I saw Randy. I told him what we had found and asked what had happened. He said it was no one of my business. And then he walked away. Our discipling relationship ended right there. I've never seen Randy since (he did a good job of avoiding me at work).

I tell you this story to emphasize my point. There is no magic formula when choosing someone to disciple. Everything indicated that Randy was an excellent guy to invest in. Even after thinking it through, over and over again, I couldn't think of any warning sign that I might have missed. I just got burned, my wife got burned, and we, for a time, felt that we would never again let anyone into our home.

Things like this happen. I suspect that every man who has discipled at least ten men can point to one of them who didn't live up to our expectations. Not that there's something wrong with our expectations. There's something wrong with some men who sin, and they won't stop sinning until they reach eternity.

There are some old books on disciple-making that encourage us to look for a F.A.T. man. Someone who is Faithful, Available, and Teachable. It's a nice acronym, but unfortunately, it's not always useful.

When we begin to disciple a man, he generally isn't faithful, especially if he's a new believer. If these guys were always available, I wouldn't be addressing how to know who to disciple. And I've found that men are teachable only to a certain point. As long as they desire the content being taught, they will learn from you. But when you touch a sensitive area in their life, they might just walk away, just like Randy did.

If one of the men you've discipled has been absent or resistant, do what you can. Maybe you're scratching where he doesn't itch. But if your efforts are consistently repelled, move on to someone else who wants help. As an old mentor of mine says, "Smile. Be gracious. Do the will of God."

As Leroy Eims mentioned in his book *The Lost Art of Disciple Making*, some men are excited to become Christians but don't want to be followed up. Some others are excited to be followed up but don't desire to be discipled. And some enjoyed being discipled, but don't want to be disciple-makers. In the end, it's not about them. It's about you.

Do what you can with what you've got. *You* be faithful in the small things, and God will give you bigger things over time. But always remember that men will drop out of the race at any time and there's nothing *you* can do to prevent it.

CHAPTER 26

Is It Okay to Disciple Someone Totally Different from Me?

This question can come from two different perspectives. That of personality, and that of doctrine. Let's address the doctrine view first.

Doctrine can have a broad meaning in the Church. There are *core* doctrines. These are things that we must agree with to be considered a true Christian. For example, the divinity of Jesus Christ is a core doctrine. Someone may believe that Jesus was not God, but simply a wise teacher. That belief does not fit into orthodox Christianity. Early church leaders came together to discuss ideas like this. Those who did not agree with the core doctrines were condemned as heretics – non-believers. These people may be more prevalent than we realize.

Let's say the person you want to disciple is a new believer. He probably hasn't had much exposure to these core doctrines. He probably has a general idea of Jesus and His death on the cross. He believes in God but may not be able to list God's attributes.

It seems new believers have more exposure to peripheral doctrines. These come from the people who have been talking to the person even before he comes to faith. These are areas that someone teaches an idea as a doctrine when it may be more of a preference. Every Christian should be baptized (that's a core doctrine). How baptism is accomplished is more of a preference. As an infant, child, or adult? By sprinkling, pouring, or immersion?

Perhaps you did not lead this new believer to Christ. Maybe you met after he began to walk with Christ. The person who led him to Christ may have come from a Pentecostal or deliverance background. You may not be Pentecostal, and you might have some well-thought-through doctrine regarding the activity of the Holy Spirit. This really does not exclude you from discipling this new believer.

The first steps of discipling, often called follow-up*, don't focus on these things. (Although it may occur within a Pentecostal church.) Our goals in follow-up are to help a new believer be sure of salvation, begin to walk with Christ, begin to feed on the Word, and to develop in prayer. Whether he prays with his hands folded or in the air doesn't matter in the basics*. We want him to pray!

Side note: Many people have asked for help in following-up a new believer. Another one of my books speaks directly to that. It's simply too large a topic to add to this book. However, in the back of this book is information about the book on follow-up. If you send me your email address through the link on that page, I will send you a copy of the book. I will make the ebook version to be free for anyone on that list!

Another way we may be different is in our personalities. I find this area much more challenging when making a disciple. We all know how personalities can clash. We all know about "chemistry" – when people just click, not don't click at all. We don't need to be married very long to understand chemistry doesn't override everything else. If there's no chemistry and that click isn't happening, think about who you know who might make a better connection. Consider introducing them to each other. It's more important that the young believer is discipled than that you get credit for it.

Some personality issues can make discipling hard to accomplish. Let me address two that I have seen increasingly in the last generation: mental and relational issues.

Depression is on the rise, along with its related problems. I recently heard U.S. Senator Ben Sasse speak about a decline in the life expectancy of Americans. He pointed out that suicide and drug-overdose have been the primary causes for this drop. Social media often contains posts about depression. Social media bullying has been blamed for increased suicide among teens.

New believers can particularly struggle here. They may have been led to believe that coming to Jesus will heal all their ills. While there is much joy found in the new life with Christ, clinical depression may still exist. When they continue to feel depressed, their faith may dwindle.

It is important that when we disciple someone with depression, we do not make promises that don't come from God's Word. Jesus did say that He came to provide us with abundant life. And he healed many of their illnesses. Yet, he didn't heal everyone. You can pray, but you can't promise physical or mental healing.

Instead, we need to keep our focus on discipling a new believer in the faith. When depression arises, we should acknowledge it and point to the right help – a licensed, qualified counselor. In all likelihood, you are not that type of counselor.

Another problem, particularly among a growing number of young men, is referred to as "daddy issues." Millions of men today have grown up with an absent or abnormal relationship with their fathers. When we begin to disciple someone, we take on the role of a spiritual father. It can be easy to move from a focus of discipling to becoming a surrogate father. Don't do that!

For women reading this book, you also know that daddy issues can affect the way someone relates to you. But you may not feel the full impact of this because you're not trying to fill a father's shoes. At least I hope you're not! However, there can be similar issues for women caused by an absent father or a poor husband. My point is that helping someone with this is *not* discipling.

When we disciple someone, we need to set personal boundaries. Care should be taken that we don't become counselors. Let counselors counsel. You disciple!

One of the guys I discipled began to help a younger guy with daddy issues. I learned that over some time, there was less discipling and more counseling. While the younger guy was feeling better about himself, he was still missing the basic spiritual disciplines he needed to grow on his own. Because the discipling relationship morphed into a counseling relationship.

Don't fall for the idea that someone needs to work out all their emotional/mental problems before he can be discipled. There's no truth to that. And being discipled may have a positive effect on his mental health.

I want to bring up another area where we may experience differences in discipling. I believe as our nation becomes more diverse, we will experience this more often. It's the issue of worldview.

I'm not talking about a Christian worldview versus a non-Christian worldview. Instead, I'm talking about three different ways of seeing and relating to our world Ways that are passed on from the dominant culture.

Most white Americans are influenced by a guilt-innocence worldview. It's the idea that someone does something wrong that makes them guilty. That invokes a penalty. We can even see this in the way we present the gospel.

Most of us are aware that Chinese and Japanese people have a different worldview – one of honor-shame. They strive to maintain honor and not shame the family name. The way they respond to the gospel is not usually based on a guilt-innocence view, but honor-shame.

A third view is fear-power. We see this primarily in Africa and South America, or people who grew up there. We also see this in Pentecostal-type churches. There is a fear of evil. This evil is often spiritual in nature. A stronger spiritual power is needed to overcome evil.[50]

My point is this. Sociologists believe younger generations in America are moving toward an honor-shame type of worldview.[51] And our next-door neighbors and co-workers may come from different worldviews than we do. Approaching them from a purely guilt-innocence view isn't helpful. Our discipling efforts will need to take these differences into consideration to disciple effectively.

As you disciple more people, you will learn to be more flexible with these differences. You will know when to point toward other resources for the complete development of someone. We don't usually have the luxury of choosing someone to disciple who is just like us. We can't administer a personality test to find an exact match – there won't be one.

As disciple-makers, we need to modify our approach to meet the needs of the younger believer. Paul points out in Romans 15: 1-2 that we need to bear with weaker believers. Sometimes it's not comfortable helping someone become a disciple when there are any (or all) of these differences. But it's worth it!

---

[50] Read more about these three worldviews in *The 3-D Gospel* by Jayson Georges (Timē Press, 2014).

[51] See "The Rise of Shame in America" on HonorShame. Accessed on October 2, 2019 at: http://honorshame.com/rise-shame-america/

CHAPTER 27

How Do I Ask to Disciple Someone?

First, let me quote the full question as it was given. "Is it appropriate/wise to ask, 'Would you like to be discipled?' Or is it better to ask, 'Would you like to meet regularly to study & discuss the things of God?' The question comes from a friend who has been told that the second option is the better one. I would agree that it is better than the first, but it's certainly not the best. Let's start with the first question.

The problem with this first question is the word "discipled." Yes, I know this entire book is about the idea. But many people don't have a clue what you mean when you ask that. In 2015, the Barna research group published data about what terms people were most likely to use to describe spiritual growth.

Barna reports, "The most preferred term was 'becoming more Christ-like' (selected by 43% of respondents), followed by 'spiritual growth' (31%), and 'spiritual journey' (28%)." Only 18% of people used the word "discipleship," and apparently, no one preferred the terms "disciple" or "disciple-making."[52]

So, there's a good chance the person you are talking to doesn't understand the first question. The exception might be when the two of you are involved in a discipling ministry. Both the Navigators and

---

[52] "New Research on the State of Discipleship." Accessed on June 24, 2019 at: https://www.barna.com/research/new-research-on-the-state-of-discipleship/.

Cru both use this term in college and military contexts, so it's better understood in these ministries.

On to the second question, which is better since it describes what you would be doing. Meeting regularly, studying, and talking are all normal concepts in our understanding. Anyone should have an idea of what you're asking with this first question. There might be some question about what you'd be studying, but that would easily come out.

Also open for discussion is what is meant by "regularly." We might assume that that means once a week. Maybe every other week. But I've known some hard-charging fellows who believe it's best to meet several times a week. Maybe in college, that pace would work. But in the work world, people just don't have that kind of time. Especially when they are married and have children.

It's easy enough to talk about how often you both are available. Working out the details shouldn't take long. But there's a problem lurking underneath there that you need to consider.

There have been several times when I asked someone to meet with me weekly. It made sense. That's exactly what I was asked to do as a young Christian. While I was in the U.S. Army, keeping my commitments was instilled deeply into my character. You always did what you agreed to. But less than one percent of the population has been in the military. That means you have a 99% chance of people thinking differently—and being less committal.

Before you rearrange your calendar for the next year with weekly meetings, try this. Look for a man that you think you'd like to meet with. Then ask him to meet with you – once. Yes, just once. Maybe over coffee. You should have a few key questions for him or ask him to share his testimony. Several things can happen in this first meeting.

Believe it or not, you might find out that this guy isn't a Christian yet. That doesn't mean that you shouldn't meet with him, but it will look different. Maybe you ask him to read a chapter of a Gospel (Mark is a good place to start). Have him write down any questions or interesting thoughts. Talk about those things. But you can't disciple a non-Christian. Your approach must be different.

Maybe he is a Christian. Good job making it through that sniff test! Yet, you might find out that there's no chemistry working in your favor. It's okay to admit that you can't minister to every guy who comes along. I run into a lot of fellows who work with computers: maintenance, installation, and programming. I find these guys are quite different from me. But I know a couple other guys who are very similar. It's better to pass on a guy like that to another man rather than to fail to make a solid connection. Although the older I get, the easier it seems to be to connect with people "unlike" me.

There's another "chemistry" issue that you might come across. Brain chemistry; or in other words, having issues with their mental health. When someone is struggling with, let's say, depression, you'll find there may be little that you can do in the way of discipling. Worse, you may find that the guy just wants to download all his woes on you. You don't want to commit to meet with someone who simply can't focus on the topics at hand. He needs a counselor – and that's not you (in most cases).

And, finally, here's the kicker. What do you do if you make a commitment a meet regularly, and then you find out the guy isn't committed? Part of discipling a guy is showing him how to be committed – a man of his word. You can show that trait. But if he doesn't have it, you'll get frustrated pretty quickly.

So, here's a better option. Ask to meet once. Get a lay of the land. Where's the guy at. I have a few exploratory questions that I use to help me assess where a guy is. In my answer to "How do I start discipling someone?" (see the next chapter), I give one of those questions that uses a 1-to-10 scale.

Here's a humdinger of another exploratory question I would encourage you to use. "What are the three most important things that someone should know about you?" Be ready to get a puzzled look with this question. I'm often told that no one has ever asked a question like that before. I've had a few guys who simply couldn't answer it. Some could give one or two responses, but not a third. Some needed to have time to think about it. And it's a great time to schedule another meeting to learn the answer next time.

The answers to this question give you a key to this man's life. (If you want to go through that door!) I recently got this response when I asked someone that question: "My name, my work, and where I'm from. If one of the three most important things about him doesn't include something spiritual, you might want to look elsewhere. Love the guy. Be friendly. But you probably don't have a man to disciple. Or, you may want to talk about the gospel. From there, if he is a Christian, you might have an opportunity to do some basic follow-up* first.

When I have a first meeting that was good – in both directions – I will ask to meet again. I push the second meeting out for two or three weeks. Asking to meet again "next week" begins to set a pattern that you may not be willing to keep. Plus, people *are* busy.

A third and fourth meeting can follow, on an irregular basis. With each meeting, get to know one another more. Did you get that? You get to know him, and you need to let him get to know you. This is not a parent-child or teacher/student interaction. Share what you've been getting out of your devotional time. How does he respond to what you share? Share how you've been applying a passage of Scripture to your family or work life. Does that pique his interest?

Once you've had several meetings like this, you'll be able to judge whether to offer to do something more regular. That's when you might go to the question about meeting regularly. But if you've got a live one, he might even ask you first!

How Do I Start Discipling Someone?

What a great question! I'm assuming this is asking about starting a discipling relationship, not about what materials you might use. There's a question about materials deeper in this book (over in chapter 32).

There are two ways to begin discipling someone: intentionally or organically. Perhaps a third way is to let things seem like they're organic when they are actually intentional! Let's talk about the intentional aspect first.

By intentional, I mean that someone starts to talk about discipling. Some guys may ask you directly. A few may hint at it. You may ask some others. But be careful with starting with the word "disciple."

Many people currently in their 20s and even in their early 30s tend to use the word "mentor," not "disciple." They may also assume that only an older person can be a mentor. ("Older" is a relative term when you're only 21 years old!) What I'm getting at here is that you need to use the same language as they do.

If they use the word mentor, it's worth your while to explore what that means to them. Some colleges have programs where a junior or senior will mentor a freshman or sophomore. Some college ministries do use the term disciple, but it may mean something a little less than what you have in mind.

One of the guys I was mentoring wanted to disciple someone. He found several men who he thought were not as mature as him in their faith. He then asked them, one by one, if they would like to be discipled. Every one of them said, "No." I had to point out to him that I never asked him into that kind of relationship. We grew into it. It was organic in its beginning and became intentional as it progressed.

That leads to the idea of organically discipling someone. Here's a related story. I met an Air Force officer on a camping trip, and we got along quite well. I asked him if we might be able to get coffee or a meal at some point. He declined the offer because his job was consuming him.

I continued to ask for a 30-minute slot with him – I offered to drive to his area – and he eventually said, "Yes." It was a quick 30 minutes. I made sure that I got him back to work on time. But we enjoyed it and agreed to try again – in a month!

After several months of 30-minute lunches, we started to meet a little more often. He somehow found a way to meet every two to three weeks! During those quick lunches, I often had the food ready for him when he got there. And occasionally we went for 45 minutes. After six months, at the end of a meeting together, came what I was looking for! He asked, "We're going to do this every week, right?" Six months! But it was so worth it.

There's an intentional method to this organic model. When you meet someone who seems to be someone you could invest in, start by just talking where you are. Whether at church, work, or some location that you both frequent like your kids' sports meetings. Maybe you do that twice, then ask to get some coffee. Yeah, that might sound like asking a girl that you're interested in out for a first date! It is similar, but with different intentions.

During that first meeting, get to know the man. Ask questions; find out about his story. Most 20- and 30-year-olds love to tell their stories. Actually, everybody likes to talk about themselves.

I have some key questions that I will ask at the first or second meeting. As we talk about his faith, I will ask about his current walk with Christ. But I do it in a way that most guys have never considered before. I ask a "scale question." Here it is:

"On a scale of one to ten; one is a brand-new believer, and ten is Billy Graham (or some other well-known Christian leader), where would you put yourself on that scale?" Some guys may struggle with the scale being too abstract; they might want something more objective. But press that they just give you an answer.

The answer itself doesn't make a lot of difference, because you're going to ask a follow-up question. (Most guys, by the way, will rate themselves a six.) The follow-up question is the most important part. I phrase it like this:

"So, you're a six. What would be one thing (if you had it, or did it, or knew it) that all by itself would take you from a six to a seven?" Expect some quiet while they think it over, but a few guys will answer quickly. The answer you get can reveal an area of the man's life that he feels he could benefit from—if he somehow builds it up.

Don't be surprised if you get an answer about the Bible – reading it, knowing more, understanding. I find that around half the guys that I ask will give a Bible type of answer, no matter what number they gave for their rating. I even had a guy who rated himself as a ten who then told me that he had never read the Bible—at all. Keep your poker face, because some responses will shock you!

Regardless of the answer you get, your reply should be, "I can help you with that." If you have an immediate tidbit to share, do that. But offer to meet again to talk more about how he can develop in that area. When you help a guy in one or two areas that he feels he needs help in, you will be able to speak into other things in his life.

Set your next meeting for about two weeks forward. That gives you time to think through and pray through the next steps. You might have something that he could read in the meantime that can begin to set the stage. I keep several small digital items on a cloud drive so that I can send someone a pdf document. (That also gives me a little more contact information!)

Allow the relationship to be one built on helping him in the areas that *he* wants help with. As you succeed with those areas, you will be able to address areas that he hasn't mentioned and may not even be aware of.

One word of caution about how you present the idea of meeting together. Until you know for sure what you're getting into, only schedule one meeting at a time. Here's another story.

I had been working with a computer technician (I'll call him Jeff), who felt like he was ready to start helping someone else. And one day, he excitedly told me he had found a guy – a high school senior from our church. They set up to meet at a burger joint every Wednesday after work and school.

About two months into their meetings, Jeff told me that he had a problem and didn't know how to handle it. They agreed to meet weekly, and he would buy the high schooler a burger meal. But the senior didn't seem responsive to the topics they were covering. Jeff was beginning to seriously question this fellow's faithfulness and commitment levels. As a matter of fact, Jeff felt like the high schooler was only coming for free food.

The problem was that Jeff made a commitment to meet every week and buy the burgers. He felt like there wasn't anything that he could currently help the student with. But how could he go back on his word? That wouldn't be modeling commitment.

The problem here was that Jeff made a commitment. He did that with an expectation that the emerging disciple would also be committed. That wasn't happening, and the disciple-maker felt bad about breaking his word. And so, he should.

In discipling others, we often talk about investing in faithful or reliable men. That term comes from 2 Timothy 2:2. Paul tells Timothy to commit (NASB) or invest (NIV) in faithful (NASB) or reliable (NIV) men. Paul knew that there were men out there who were not faithful. And those men are still out there today. By setting meetings one at a time, we can see if a man is worthy of the time and energy commitment, we will need to make in them. Don't dive in without knowing where you're headed!

Did I just qualify a guy with the word "worthy?" Yes, I did. There are hundreds of men out there wanting to be discipled by someone. (Just because they aren't standing in front of you with a flashing neon sign doesn't mean they're not there.) In the words of a famous preacher from Minneapolis, "Don't Waste Your Life!"

When you spin your wheels on a man who is not committed, not faithful, not teachable, you deprive these other men of getting what they are seeking to become; disciples who make disciples.

CHAPTER 29

What Do We Do in Disciple-Making?

"We are fooling ourselves if we think we are going to
produce mature and multiplying disciples by
meeting once a week over coffee or in a small group."[53]
Bob McNabb

There was more to the original question that included three activities that might occur while making disciples. They were: "Read the Word? Read a book? Spend time together?" You get the idea from those activities that the question deals with how we go about discipling, not what topics we cover.

Jesus gave us a goal for disciple-making: that the disciple becomes like the teacher (Matthew 10:25 and Luke 6:40). Much of this is done the way the Apostle Paul practiced making disciples. In 1 Corinthians 11:1, he urged people to imitate him. All on the precept that he was imitating Christ.

There's no way someone can imitate you if you don't spend time with them. So that last idea is quite valid. But what you do when you're spending time together is of utmost importance. If all you're doing in talking about the last sports event, there won't be much to imitate. So, what should you do while you're spending time together?

---

[53] Bob McNabb, Spiritual Multiplication in the Real World (Hoover, AL: Multiplication Press, 2013), 121.

The first rule of great disciple-making is to learn as much as you can about your man. This shouldn't be a foreign concept. Football coaches will show videos of the opposing team to learn their strengths and weaknesses. Boxers and their coaches watch other boxers for their stance, footwork, and punch. We're not looking to knock someone out, but we do want to learn about them so that they can win the prize of faith (1 Corinthians 9:24).

Two areas are critical in knowing your man: his personal needs and his learning style. A third area that will come along after some time is his love language. Here are some stories to flesh out those points.

A man I was discipling said that he was spending time with men, but they were not responding to him. So, I decided to go spy on him – yep, literally spy. I watched him "spend time" with a guy who was working on his car. The guy was moving around the engine and beneath the car. But my disciple never once offered to help – not even to hand him a wrench. This poor guy did not need someone to stand over him and talk. He needed someone to help with the oil change!

You may not see helping with an oil change as a spiritual need, and it probably isn't. But we do need to see the obvious needs in someone's life. If we can't help with the obvious, how can we help with deeper things?

My wife talked with me once about leaving a church we had gone to for several years. She said she wasn't getting anything out of the sermons. (I thought they were great!) But her comment was, "He never tells me what to do."

I talked with the pastor a couple weeks later. I asked him how he develops his sermons. He told me that adults at the church had an average master's level of education. He crafted his sermons to emphasize theory. He assumed most people would take that theory and decide what to do. When I told him that my wife wanted to know what to do, he said, "Oh, I could never do that."

This one-approach-fits-all way of preaching led to our leaving that church for one where my wife could flourish. And that gave me a lesson on how people learn. There simply isn't a one-size-fits-all tactic. We need to know the person we're discipling, so we can teach in a way that is best for them. That means we spend a little more effort preparing for our time together. And we may even set aside what we prepare when we realize it's not the best thing for him—at least not for now.

And finally, something on love languages. My father used to talk about all the things he bought for me. Tricycles, bicycles, mini-bikes, footballs, baseballs, and gloves you name it he bought it. It proved his love for me – in his eyes. But it was my aunt who took the time to teach me to ride the bike and catch the ball. Do you see the conflict in love language? My father was a gift-giver when I needed quality time. And because my aunt "talked" my love language, she had more impact on my childhood.

So again, the most important thing you can do in disciple-making is getting to know your man. That will require spending time together. Time to observe, time to ask personal questions, time to see him in action.

By the way, personal questions may not work in budding discipling meetings. You work into those as the relationship develops depth. When in doubt, ask. Last month, I attended a conference and sat at a table with a man from South Africa. We talked about a lot of things. As we were saying goodbye, I felt a hug was appropriate. But I asked!

I asked him how people say goodbye in South Africa. Do they shake hands, wave goodbye, hug? I was told that it's not culturally appropriate to hug someone outside your family or a very intimate friend. However, he felt our time together was strong enough to allow a hug – a side hug with a handshake between us. It's best to ask when in doubt!

For a time, Christians used to talk about "loving on someone." A pastor friend in Arkansas still uses the term and gets some odd looks from others unfamiliar with it. We do want to "love on" our disciples. But we need to love in such a way that *they* feel loved, not us. If a man doesn't feel loved after meeting with you, you'll probably lose him.

If you didn't catch it the last two times, let me say this once again. The most important thing you can do in discipling a man is to get to know him.

Beyond that comes some of the specific *whats* of discipling. Do we do a Bible study? Read our Bibles together? Pray together. Read a popular Christian book (or business book)? Two things help you make this decision. What you know about your man and what you want to see developed in his life. (He should also want to develop the same thing in his life.)

As I got to know one guy, a college graduate, I learned that he has dyslexia. He simply can't read the way I do. How did he get through college? He bought electronic books and used a computer application that read each ebook to him. He still does the same thing with other books. And he says, "I read a book on the way to work yesterday." He didn't read it, he listened to it.

So, when I'm going to recommend a book for him, I check to see if there's an ebook or audio version before I bring it up. And to protect his dignity, I would never ask him to read a portion of Scripture with me. I must rely on his visual and audible skills to disciple him. And let me assure you that there are far more of these guys out there than we realize.

As you get to know your man and develop a plan of topics to cover, the doing falls in place. I do not intend, in this book, to spell out a plan or endorse materials to use. Materials are plentiful, and none of them seem to be foolproof. I will give you a general plan with the next question.

CHAPTER 30

Is It Best to Disciple One-on-One or in Small Groups?

"Certainly the emphasis should be on the individual,
for we find that people differ and at times
need individual care to meet their need."[54]
Charles Riggs

I'm not very good at an either-or type of question. I often go for the both-and type of answers. And this will be one of those times. Discipling is done in both ways, but it has the best results in one. The quote above from Charlie Riggs, the Director of Counseling and Follow-Up for the Billy Graham Crusade team, probably reveals my answer.

My Christian walk has been most influenced by man-to-man interactions. I heard the gospel in a one-on-one context. We had been in a small group meeting, but when it came time to hear the gospel, it was personalized to me. I learned later that the small group was praying for me as I heard the gospel.

Once I became a Christian, I continued to go to group meetings. There was a Bible study of around eight guys. There was a larger

---

[54] Quoted from the Forward by Charles Riggs. Waylon Moore. *New Testament Follow-Up for Pastors and Laymen: How to Conserve, Mature, and Multiply Converts* (Grand Rapids: Wm. B. Eerdmans Company, 1963), 10.

monthly meeting with around fifty to sixty people. And there was the Army chapel with around a hundred people. In each of these places, I heard Bible teaching. But it was in the small group where I was personally encouraged in my growth.

I want to be clear that there was growth, but most of it did not come from the groups, large or small, that I attended. The man who led me to Christ spent time with me one-on-one. It was during these times that I could ask questions about what I had heard. I could ask what he was doing in an area I was addressing. And more often than not, he often brought up subjects, ideas, or methods that I had never considered or heard of. (The larger the group, the less likely you are to hear about sensitive topics – topics that can make or break your spiritual walk if not addressed.)

I'm a fan of small groups. I grew up in them. But they simply don't meet all your needs. Think about it this way. Not even fifty years ago, churches only had large group worship services. A church small group was unheard of (other than a Sunday school class).

Today, you would be hard-pressed to find a church that doesn't have some kind of small group meeting. Some have abandoned adult Sunday school classes altogether. Weekly small groups, mostly in homes, have replaced them. My point is that the church might be behind "best practices." They simply haven't caught on to the idea of one-on-one discipling yet. After all, how long did it take for small groups to catch on? 1,900 years? (Yes; John Wesley developed a small group model in the late 1700s in England.)

Could it be that one-on-one was the predominant discipling method in first-century Christianity? But the focus quickly changed to small groups (house churches), that eventually changed to large church buildings? And is the pendulum now swinging back to the original method?

But "Wait," you say. Jesus himself discipled in small groups. He had the twelve apostles, and they were always with him. (Do you ever wonder where all thirteen of them slept at night?)

"Yes," I say, to an extent. The Gospels describe Jesus ministering in groups, big and small. Even when he was addressing one person, it was often within earshot of others. There was Zacchaeus, the woman caught in adultery, the Roman centurion, and a host of others.

But hold on! There was also the woman at the well. And Nicodemus, alone together at night. Did you ever wonder how these few stories of one-on-one conversations got into our Bibles? Jesus must have relayed the details after they happened. Just like he would have had to when he was tempted in the wilderness. We can't assume that there were no other one-on-one interactions with Jesus. The Apostle John said that many things didn't get written down.

In the same way, we might think Paul did all his discipling in some type of group setting. He writes, "The things you heard from me *in the presence of many witnesses...*" (2 Timothy 2:2). If I'm sitting in Starbucks talking directly to you, am I not in the presence of many witnesses? Just today, as I am editing this page, a woman approached me and a friend meeting one-to-one in a coffee shop in Coos Bay, Oregon, and asked me to explain what she overheard me saying. She must have been one of those many witnesses!

Jesus did, in fact, do most of his teaching in groups. From 5,000 men on a hillside to inside a small village synagogue. It's interesting, though, that the explanations of his teaching were to a smaller group (Mark 4:10). And sometimes, he only had three guys with him (poor brother Andrew! — Matthew 17:1). Yet there are also times when he is directly speaking only to one of those eleven or twelve men.

We simply can't assume that because the Bible doesn't mention more one-on-one talks that they didn't happen. Any more than we can assume that the disciples never went home to sleep. Peter, after all, did have a wife (as proved by a sick mother-in-law). That means he probably also had kids. These details weren't written because the Gospel writers had a specific message that didn't include Peter's family. The Gospels weren't meant to be a social history, or a church administration manual, or a disciple-making handbook.

Think about mental health counseling. We can see the usefulness of both one-on-one and small group meetings. Being in a group helps me know I'm not the only one struggling with a common problem. But I also need to have some one-on-one therapy time with a counselor to help me work through deep issues. (Sorry, if you're reading into this; Nope! While I use the first person here, I don't actually go to a counseling group.) Most of us wouldn't broadcast those issues to a group. And we might think someone who does is socially awkward.

While I'm on that idea of counseling, I want to bring up the purpose of a small group. I read a book years ago on small groups. I think it was Rick Howerton's *A Different Kind of Tribe*. He described four different primary purposes for a group. Communal, Missional, Restorational, and Theological.

Without explaining the differences, I want to say that not every small group has the set purpose of making disciples. A small group that focuses on counseling wants to bring restoration to its members. A theological group is committed to learning, usually through Bible study. While these groups may sometimes delve into the other three purposes, they always return to the primary one.

So, a community group *might* be the closest to a discipling group. One that is seeking to make disciples of its members. If they don't get distracted by the potluck supper, and singing, and updates on family life, and, oh, it's late, we need to get the kids home to bed.

I have been in some community groups where people "speak into" the lives of others. This type of accountability often goes beyond the weekly meeting. There are phone calls or text messages, but I've never heard of a group phone call for this. Those are always one-on-one.

On a related thought, have you ever thought about why Jesus explained the process for dealing with sin the way that he did (Matthew 18:15-17)? He talked about going to someone and talking about the issue between you—one-to-one. If that didn't work, do it again with one or two other people with you. Only if that doesn't work should you bring it to a larger group. Many personal areas that are best dealt with one-on-one. The group, in this case, a church, is involved at the end of the process. And that involves potential discipline.

Now, let me get to a couple reasons I prefer one-on-one discipling. The first one is expediency. The second is privacy.

We all know that adage that too many cooks spoil the broth. When I'm meeting one-on-one, I can get right to the heart of the issue. It's not just about sin. It could be any area that a person needs to grow in; any of those traits of a disciple from Section One.

Small groups can be potential traps. There's a mixture of spiritual maturity. I begin to address an issue, and someone else pipes up with a question or argument. I wind up explaining an idea or defending myself to that person instead of discipling the first guy.

With one-on-one, I address only the issue with the individual man. I answer his questions or address his push back. Not somebody else's. And the key is that I want to help that faithful man. The guy who has already expressed an interest in being a disciple. And I can usually do that in thirty minutes instead of an entire evening with a group.

I find that I can disciple a man in much less time when I focus just on him. That's not to devalue the group. But the need to make disciples is critical. And after forty-five years, I can say the best way to make a disciple who can then make another disciple is by the one-to-one method.

is critical. And after forty-five years, I can say the best way to make a disciple who can then make another disciple is by the one-to-one method.

CHAPTER 31

Should Disciple-Making Be Done Using the Bible Only?

As I think back over 40 years of making disciples, I am surprised at how often this question comes up. Of course, the Bible is the primary source for discipling. But it isn't the only source. Let me give you a personal example.

When I came to Christ, I had never read the Bible even though I had one (maybe two). I didn't know how to approach this holy book. When I was a child, many homes had a large Bible with colorful pictures inside sat on a coffee table in every living room. You never moved it, or even touched it. Was there a certain way to carry it? Did I have to put it on the top of a stack of other books? Was I allowed to use a highlighter or underline something?

The fellow who led me to Christ understood that I knew nothing. Slowly he gave me pointers on what to do, how to read, where to read. I even noticed that he underlined in his Bible. So, I learned from his example that it was okay. But maybe not for the coffee table edition!

This personal example should start to answer the question. The Bible itself doesn't give me any of these answers. There are a lot of things about being a disciple that the Bible doesn't address. We either must be told by someone or read about it somewhere else.

I've seen the acronym B.I.B.L.E. It stands for "Basic Instructions Before Leaving Earth." If I relied solely on my Bible for all the instructions I needed before I died, I'd be in trouble. There are many things in the Bible that the writers assumed you already knew. How do you learn them if not from outside the Bible?

Still not convinced? How did you learn to do inductive Bible study? Maybe not something as fancy as inductive. Maybe just a fill-in-the-blank format. Your Bible doesn't teach you how to do that. The Bible does talk about studying, but it doesn't tell you how. We learn that from somewhere else. Through people, podcasts, or paperbacks.

Gordon Fee wrote a book titled, *How to Read the Bible for Everything It's Worth*. I keep two copies so I can offer one to others to help them grow in their understanding of God's Word. I can sit for several hours explaining things. Or I can hand them a book, and they can go through on their time.

It's helpful for someone to learn how to read his Bible from a book. And by doing so, I am helping him meet the traits of a disciple.

Another personal example. As a young Christian, my disciple-maker would bring cassette tapes for us to listen to together. The messages were always Bible-based, with many verses quoted. But it was the explanation that helped me. Even more than that, my friend would stop the tape and ask my thoughts. That's something that doesn't happen during a sermon at church!

Today, you might listen to a podcast or MP3 on a cell phone together. Or watch an online video. The sources are different, but the results can be the same. Hit pause and talk about key ideas. This is as much disciple-making as reading the Bible together.

Some people struggle with reading. They might have dyslexia, or they might be more auditory than visual. Many Millennials and Gen Zs have been brought up in an auditory world. They read much less than previous generations. But they listen even less than they read!

Have you noticed that movies and books are shorter than fifty years ago? With so many distractions, we need to make our points or tell our stories in shorter ways. No more one-hour sermons; most of them are now less than twenty minutes.[55] That's not something that our Bibles can tell us. It's not wrong; it's different.

---

[55] In the Soviet Union in the 1980s, Russian Christians would listen to a two-hour sermon, go home for lunch, and return for a second two-hour sermon! In Africa, some churches have two or three preachers who take turns with one-hour sermons. Even there, many American churches have reduced the sermon to under thirty minutes today.

In disciple-making, we need to learn our men as much as our message. If we can't communicate with the man, the message will be lost.

We do need to use the Bible. Doing so helps our disciple learn its value. But in today's world, we need secondary sources that will help us make a complete disciple. The traits of that disciple are found in the Bible. How to reach those traits today may need to come from outside sources. It's a both-and answer; not an either-or one.

CHAPTER 32

Is There a Curriculum I Can Use to Make Disciples?

Ah, the most often asked question! Yes, there is. But it may not be what you think you're looking for! Usually, when someone uses the word curriculum, they mean a program of study, a course or courses, materials of some kind. You're probably looking for something already put together to buy. There have been plenty of churches that have produced things to buy. Willow Creek Community Church near Chicago comes immediately to mind. I do not intend to trash talk this church, only to use it as an example.

After Willow Creek grew into a mega-church, they began to sell program materials they developed. I knew churches in Texas that styled themselves after the Willow Creek model and used their curriculum. However, after they had been selling materials, Willow Creek began to research the people attending locally.

Here are the findings in a nutshell:

> Before the research, Willow Creek had been assuming that "the more a person far from God participates in church activities, the more likely it is those activities will produce a person who loves God and loves others." However, this assumption was found to be invalid by the research. To quote the study: "Does increased attendance in ministry programs

automatically equate to spiritual growth? To be brutally honest: it does not." [56]

Gary Kuhne addressed the confidence we put in curriculum to help others grow in their walk. His main point is that we lean on printed curriculum for two reasons: we feel the lack of manpower to meet one-to-one with someone, and the marketing of Christian materials implies success rates without any supporting data. We just tend to believe a publisher's anecdotal testimony about one believer's growth and assume it will work for every person. Kuhne writes, "Such advertising is a real scandal in the evangelical community and creates a critical collision of ethics for publishers and ministries that have gone overboard in their praise and confidence of such standardized curriculums." [57]

But rather than to deflate your hopes, let me point to a Bible passage that can give you some direction for "curriculum." First John 2: 12-14 (NASB) says:

> I am writing to you, little children, because *your sins have been forgiven you* for His name's sake. I am writing to you, fathers, because you know Him who has been from the beginning. I am writing to you, young men, because you have overcome the evil one. I have written to you, children, because *you know the Father.* I have written to you, fathers, because you know Him who has been from the beginning. I have written to you, young men, because you are strong, and *the word of God abides in you*, and you have overcome the evil one. [Emphasis is mine]

John says that he is writing to little children, children, young men, and fathers. (Read more about these groups in Chapter 35 about the stages of disciple-making.) What's important for us to see is what he was writing to each of these groups.

He said in verse twelve that he was writing to little children. He also said it was because their sins are forgiven. Now grab your Bible and read everything above verse twelve. Notice anything? What he wrote at the beginning of this letter was about sin and forgiveness. There's some curriculum for a new believer!

---

56 Russ Rainey. "Summary of the Willow Creek REVEAL Study" on The Christian Coaching Center. Accessed on July 19, 2019 at: http://www. christiancoachingcenter.org/index.php/russ-rainey/coachingchurch2/

57 Gary Kuhne. *Follow-up Dynamics: A Handbook for the Personal Follow-up of New Christians.* North East, PA: Ministry Dynamics Press, 1999.

I will give you more about this in my answer about the stages of disciple-making. But for now, I would direct you to materials that are already available that can be used to:

- Assure the new believer of forgiveness, salvation, victory over temptation, and guidance (What is commonly referred to as follow-up*)
- Help the growing believer develop a personal relationship with God through Bible intake and prayer
- Encourage disciples to abide in the Word to make them strong against the evil one

We have already seen that one of the traits of a disciple is that he abides in God's Word. This goes far beyond listening to a weekly sermon. Even adding a weekly Bible study group doesn't equate to abiding. To make disciples, we must teach and emphasize the basics*. Having a grasp on these basics will result in mature believers who can reproduce themselves in the lives of others. Then we will have disciples who make disciples!

CHAPTER 33

How Long Does Disciple-Making Take?

Good question—because it's good to know what you're committing yourself to.[58] I'm not sure we can get this down to a specific amount of time. Everybody is different. Some grow very quickly; others take their own sweet time. It does depend on the commitment level of the emerging disciple*. Your discipling methods may also have an impact on time. But I think the primary impact today is the culture that we live in.

Dawson Trotman was the founder of a disciple-making ministry. He gave a message entitled "Born to Reproduce" in the 1950s. Back then, he felt that most people could meet the profile of a disciple in six months. LeRoy Eims personally knew Dawson. They shared much of the same vision. Yet when LeRoy wrote a book on disciple-making in the mid-1980s, he thought it could take between three and four years. In thirty years, the amount of time increased by 300 percent!

Many seasoned disciple-makers that I talk with today have doubled that again. We think that it now takes up to seven years to produce a disciple at the same level as the 1950s! What happened?

Watch an episode of *Leave It to Beaver* or *Father Knows Best* from the 1950s. (Search for them on YouTube.com.) We can easily see that our world has drastically changed from what is portrayed on these

---

[58] The person you are discipling does NOT need to be told that it might take seven years or more. Very few people would commit to something that seems so far off. Don't shoot yourself in the foot!

"quaint" TV shows from that era. There were virtues back then that escape television programming today.

In 1975, James Engel wrote the book *What's Gone Wrong with the Harvest*. He pointed to changes occurring in our culture that made it harder to share the gospel. People didn't have the same starting block from a generation before. Engel was looking at people making gospel decisions.[59] Christians are living in this same cultural shift. Most of us have been born into it. And it affects how quickly someone becomes a disciple.

This means there are more difficult issues that a new believer encounters today. The public-school system now teaches children a morality that excludes God. By April 1966, even Time Magazine asked the question, "Is God Dead?" on their front cover.[60] As Western society became more post-modern, it began to embrace relativism.

This way of thinking then entered mainline churches. In October 1965, Time Magazine published a report on mainline theologians who were writing God out of theology. And people began to believe that all religions are going up the same mountain - we're just using different paths. These now-entrenched cultural influences make being a disciple who follows the commands of Christ much harder today.

Another area that has changed is the way we view authority. I joined the U.S. Army in 1973. Many people in America were actively protesting the Vietnam Conflict. But there was still deference given to most positions of authority. Today, our culture teaches us to question all authorities, especially law enforcement members. The younger generations have been taught to never blindly follow anyone and following implies obeying someone.

If it does take seven years to make a disciple, we've got our work cut out for us. The old model of reaching the world in less than 20 years doesn't work anymore.[61] I, for one, am still committed to

---

[59] James Engel and Wilbert Norton. What's Gone Wrong with the Harvest? A Communication Strategy for the Church and World Evangelism (Grand Rapids: Zondervan Publishing House, 1975).

[60] "Time Magazine Cover: Is God Dead?" Time, 1966-04-08.

[61] Many disciple-makers share a model of spiritual multiplication by reaching one person and discipling them over a one-year period. Then the two of you, each reach one for another year. Then the four reach four more. This multiplies out over 18 years to reach and disciple the entire population of the planet. See "Movement Math" by Jay Lorenzen found at: http://onmovements.com/?p=101 (accessed on June 7, 2019).

spiritual multiplication. Yet, I realize we need new models and processes to implement the spiritual truth of 2 Timothy 2:2.

Cultural changes aren't our only hurdles. Americans are moving every five years on average. That means, on average, you will not fully disciple anyone! Discipling now becomes something that at least two or three people are doing in the life of one person. Most of these disciple-makers do not know one another and may feel the need to cover traits already addressed in another location. That almost makes the answer to this question a moot point.

I have been discipling men for over four decades. I did not lead most of those men to Christ. You might say I adopted them somewhere along the way. There have been men I have led to Christ. Most of them moved before they became full-fledged disciples, thanks to their military service. A couple moved away and returned, which was nice, but not the norm.

Perhaps you live in a small town where no one moves anywhere. Then you have the possibility of fully discipling one person to meet the marks of a disciple. You might even see them begin to make disciples themselves. But the U.S. Census Bureau says that 80 percent of Americans now live in urban areas.[62] And "urban" seems to mean "constantly moving!"

Make use of whatever time God has given you to invest in another person. I know men who I was able to impact in only one meeting. Others I was able to impact over a few years. Many of those I wished could stay, but they moved on, and someone else furthered their growth.

Most of us are going to work at making disciples without being able to finish the job before they move elsewhere. We will also meet people that someone else began to disciple where they lived before. We need to help each of them become mature disciples who can begin to make disciples themselves.

---

[62] See "New Census Data Show Differences Between Urban and Rural Populations" on United States Census Bureau. Accessed on June 7, 2019 at: https://www.census.gov/newsroom/press-releases/2016/cb16-210.html

How Long Before You Release a Disciple?

Related to the previous question comes this one with a slightly different bend. Rather than how long does it take, this question focuses on how long does the disciple-maker need to be involved. You might also ask how long the disciple-maker *needs* to be involved versus *wants* to be involved. Let's address that first.

I recently told one of my pastor friends at lunch that disciple-making is hard. "Absolutely," was his reply! Many of us have a natural tendency to avoid hard things in life. That's especially true if the return on investment is questionable. When discipling gets hard, we might be easily persuaded to bring our discipling relationship to an end.

The opposite can also happen. We may not feel ready to release a new disciple. They may not know everything we think they need to know. This reflects some of the helicopter parenting techniques of the 2010 decade. There's some idea that grown children aren't capable of making the right decision, so we stay involved (overly involved) to "help" them.

Here's an example of "early release" from the New Testament. The book of Acts tells the story of Timothy from Lystra in Asia Minor, joining Paul and Silas on a mission trip (Acts 16:1-4). Luke, who wrote Acts, does not tell us how much time passed, but it doesn't appear to be too much time; probably only a few months.

Acts chapter 17 tells how Paul moved on to Thessalonica and then Berea. He runs into some trouble in Berea, caused by the Jews of

Thessalonica, and had to leave town for Athens. But he left Silas and Timothy in Berea to get the little church of new believers established before they would join him later in Athens. They didn't get to Athens with him but do show up after Paul is already in Corinth.

Some people think that Paul led Timothy to Christ when he met him in Lystra (although he's already called a disciple in Acts 16:1). But only a few months later, Timothy is left behind to help establish a church with Silas. While we don't know a lot about Silas, he had only joined Paul since the beginning of this second mission trip. So, two young men with minimal experience were left on their own to care for a fledgling church. Neither of them would probably be "good enough" to do the same thing today.

Am I suggesting that most converts today are ready to be released to self-directed disciple-making ministry in just a few months? No! In question number 33, I outlined how much longer it takes to make a disciple over the past 50 years. But your disciple may be more ready than you are!

As you disciple your man, you should be able to tell what traits of a disciple he is strong in and where he needs help. You should begin to move from a primary disciple-maker role to a mentor role as he develops more of these traits. There's no simple test to confirm that he's ready. You may release one too early and then release the next too late (out of caution). This is more of an art than a science.
Jesus practiced this model of early release. He first asked his twelve disciples to follow him and learn by example. Then he gave them short trips when they could practice what they learned. When they came back, Jesus took them off to a quiet place—probably for a debriefing, as we called it in the military. Finally, after only two and a half to three years, they were released to full-time ministry. Although he promised he would be with them always (Matthew 28: 20).

Are There Stages of Disciple-Making?

Yes, there are, and we can see those stages in the Apostle John's first letter. Here's what he wrote:

> I am writing to you, *little children*, because your sins have been forgiven you for His name's sake. I am writing to you, *fathers*, because you know Him who has been from the beginning. I am writing to you, *young men*, because you have overcome the evil one. I have written to you, *children*, because you know the Father. I have written to you, *fathers*, because you know Him who has been from the beginning. I have written to you, *young men*, because you are strong, and the word of God abides in you, and you have overcome the evil one. (1 John 2:12-14, NASB, italics mine)

Within the space of three verses, John mentions four stages of believers: little children, children, young men, and fathers. Please note the Bible version you use may only have three terms – children, young men, and fathers (such as the NIV). They do that to make the language easy to understand. But the original Greek text has four different words which show a difference between a little child (*teknia*) and a child (*paidia*).

Not only does John mention four groups of believers, but he also specifies what he was writing about to each group. To the youngest of the believers, little children, he wrote about forgiveness. Just look at the verses in 1 John 1. There you find not only forgiveness, but many things related to being a sinner who finds forgiveness.

I remember when I first became a Christian. I was excited about my new life. But the day came when I blatantly sinned. There was a great struggle that began in my heart and mind, down to my very soul. But very soon after that, someone shared 1 John 1:9 with me. And I came to understand that my relationship to sin was now different. I was forgiven when I simply confessed my sin. And sin was no longer my master (Romans 6:14) – Jesus was!

I believe that forgiveness is the most important topic you can cover as a disciple-maker. If a new believer doesn't get this truth in his life, his life will be a mess. I've met with far too many Christians who are still fighting a battle that Jesus already won.

Many of us refer to this early stage as "follow-up." * We follow up on someone's decision to trust Christ. We make sure they understand the decision that they just made. We work through any doubts that might come up. We point to 1 John 1:9 and explain what it means to confess – to agree with what God already knows.

Follow-up should only take a few weeks. Much of this can be covered in just a few weeks. I keep a small pocket-size notebook with me that has four assurances listed. Assurance of salvation; of forgiveness; of victory; of guidance. I list a couple verses for each topic. I sit down and have the new believer read those verses. We talk about what each verse means—mostly from his perspective, not mine. I simply ask questions to guide him in understanding the essence. And then we nail down what difference that makes in his life. Each topic can be covered in 10-to-15 minutes. (Remember babies have small stomachs!)

The next stage that John mentions is the child. Look at that Greek word *paidia*. What does it remind you of? I can't help it. I'm a Star Wars fan. Remember how Obi-Wan Kenobi called the young Anakin Skywalker "Padawan." Anakin was a young child who had Jedi abilities. But he wasn't a Jedi yet! He had to be trained.

The child-stage believer needs to be trained to know the Father. The little child learned that his bond to sin is now broken. The child now begins to learn how to have a relationship with God. That might sound funny, but many people don't know how to build a connection with God. In a world of broken homes and fuzzy spiritual thinking, each new believer needs to be taught how to begin to relate to God.

In this child phase, the Bible often calls the discipling work we do here "establishing." (Other Bible translations might use the word "completing" or "perfecting.") The Apostle Paul mentions this movement from a little child to child in Colossians 1:22-23a:

> But now he has reconciled you by Christ's physical body through death to present you holy in his sight, without blemish and free from accusation— if you continue in your faith, established and firm, and do not move from the hope held out in the gospel.

By the death of Christ, a new believer is reconciled to God. He learns that Satan can no longer accuse him of sin. He has found forgiveness. And now he continues in his new life in Christ by becoming established and firm.

We help the child-stage believer be established by helping him get into God's word. He starts to pray for himself and others. He joins a fellowship of believers – a church. And he even begins to share his new faith with others – family and friends. Some of us refer to these specific topics as "the basics." *

As the child-stage believer gets to know his Bible, he starts to understand more about God. He learns about His character – traits such as love, holiness, justice. He also begins to understand how his life should change. Some change just happens, while other change takes obedience. The old self is being put off, the new self is put on (Colossians 3:9-10). He will continue to do this for the rest of his life, but in many cases, it does get easier.

I love the third stage – young men (*neaniskos*). They are mentioned twice in 1 John 2 (13 and 14). Verse thirteen simply says they have overcome the evil one, but verse fourteen tells us why. "You are strong, and the word of God abides in you, and you have overcome the evil one" (1 John 2:14, NASB).

I'd like to point out two key thoughts here. First, it's the young men who are overcoming the evil one. That implies that the little children and children are not overcoming. I remember back when I lived in Kansas. Someone would pick on my sisters. They were usually defenseless. What did they do? They got their big brother to protect them. Young men are learning how to defend themselves and others. They're learning how to overcome. But how?

The answer is two-fold. Young men are strong, which gives them an advantage over the evil one. But it's how they become strong that's critical. They learn to abide in God's Word. This is the key difference between the child stage and the young man stage. The child is learning about God's Word. The young man is learning how to let God's Word influence every part of his life. He's learning how to use God's Word for every good work (2 Timothy 3:16). He's handling God's Word correctly (2 Timothy 2:15). God's Word is becoming a guide for every decision the young man faces. And by doing this—abiding in the Word—he has the strength to overcome the evil one.

If you ask me, I would say that the young man stage gives us a clear picture of a disciple of Jesus. He can prayerfully grasp how to apply God's Word to his life, with the help of the Holy Spirit. And by doing that, he has victory in many areas of his life. He may not be perfect. Most young men aren't. But he's moving in the right direction.

Here's one more thought. Young men can reproduce. Children can't. Children can contribute to the cause of Christ, but they simply don't have the maturity that allows them to have children of their own. In the Greek and Hebrew worlds, a young man was anywhere from a teenager to a 50-year-old. This is when they begin to marry and have children.

Once they have children, we want to see them begin to father the child. Fathers see to it that the child is raised in a way that prepares him to become an adult. And even once the young man becomes an adult, the father continues in the roles of mentoring and coaching. This is a perfect example of being a disciple-maker!

So, yes! There are stages of disciple-making. The Apostle John helps us understand those stages and gives us guidance on what to focus on when. He didn't give us specifics on how to do that. Each person may need a slightly different approach. But the general format is there.

One last thought. In a previous answer, I mentioned that some disciple-makers and equippers now think that it may take up to seven years to make a disciple. For sure, it shouldn't take 12 to 14 years to get a guy from his new birth to the young man stage. At the same time, it also doesn't have to take a full seven years to do that.

These stages do not have a hard and fast timeline that you must follow. But there is a progression. Help a little child bask in the forgiveness of the Lord and know that he can make headway over sin in his life. Then help the child with the basics of the Word, prayer, fellowship, and being a witness. Then help him abide in the Word and let him figure out how to make the Word alive and effective in his own life. No more spoon feeding or choosing what he eats. A disciple who makes disciples can feed himself!

What About Distractions?

It's good that someone realizes that there actually *are* distractions. They come in two forms: major things that can keep you from disciple-making altogether and minor things that get you off target when you are discipling. Let's immediately talk about the major things first.

Major Distractions

I was having lunch with a pastor who expressed concern that men he was trying to help had "no time to meet." What that meant was that by the time a fellow who works full-time gets home from work, helps get dinner ready, and helps clear the dishes, there was little time left in the evening. In this particular case, the man told his pastor that he *had* to be home by 7:30 p.m. to put the kids to bed – every night.

I'm going to propose that in this case, the children are a major distraction. Wait – hear me out! This fellow is saying that there isn't one evening a week when he can stay out "late" because he must be the one to put the kids to bed. Nope, his wife doesn't work an evening shift. He just decided that he will always put the kids to bed.

I have heard many men use children or their wives as a reason they cannot disciple someone or even attend a small group during the week. I understand the importance of spending time with your children – I had three of my own. But here's the stark reality: you have 18 years to spend with your children. And if you can't find a couple hours to invest in yourself or someone else, you may be drawing from an empty well when you're trying to nourish your kids.

I will come back to the first trait that we discussed on the Being a Disciple section: Luke 14:26. Note all the family members that are listed here:

> "If anyone comes to me and does not hate father and mother, wife and children, brothers and sisters—yes, even their own life—such a person cannot be my disciple."[63]

When any of these people prevent you from following Jesus – or being a disciple who makes disciples – they are a major distraction.

Work can also be another major distraction. I know a young, single military officer who never has time to meet anyone; me, his best friend, or his co-workers. He goes to the gym while it's still dark, washes up, and works until 8 or 9 p.m. at night. He even spends several hours working on most Saturdays. And here's the kicker; no one else in his unit works those kinds of hours. It's almost like he's using work to hide from life. Yes, being single can be hard and somewhat lonely, but using work to avoid being connected is similar to using work like a mind-numbing narcotic.

Work often demands more time from us than it did in the 1950s when Danny Thomas came home to his family at "the dinner hour." Yes, they actually spent an hour sitting together, having a meal, and conversation as a family. Work not only can keep us from disciple-making, but it can also keep us from our family. Double whammy!

To top that off, the Millennial Generation seems to be constantly moving from job to job. A new position in a new city offers $5,000 more a year. So off they go, constantly disconnecting from friends and potential disciples that they might invest in.[64]

Finally, and I want to be sensitive here, a third major distraction is our mental health. Every day we can read that anxiety and depression rates are skyrocketing. Having worked among military service members, I know that PTSD, left untreated or improperly treated, can significantly impair our ability to relate to others. And

---

[63] Side note! Have you ever noticed how the New International Version tries to make *almost* everything gender neutral, even when it doesn't make sense? Who has a "wife?" A person, or a man?

[64] This isn't just the Millennial Generation. It's been going on since at least the mid-1980s; enough so that sociologists have developed the term Emerging Adults for people between the ages of 19 and 29. It just so happens that is I write this that includes much of the lower half of the Millennials along with some Gen Zs.

disciple-making requires us to be able to effectively relate to one another.

Here's what I am *not* saying about mental health. I am *not* saying that someone with a psycho-social medical diagnosis cannot disciple someone else. They can, but only when properly being treated. (Treatment doesn't have to last forever in most cases.)[65] And sometimes these treated people can be the very best at discipling others with similar problems.

You may not always know that you have a mental health impairment. Sometimes even your spouse may not know or want to mention it. That's because it can grow so slowly that you don't see the difference from one day to another. So, ask a trusted friend if anything is going on in your life that might restrict your ability to relate well to others. Listen carefully and take what they have to say as helpful, not hurtful. Then get help – and help may often mean a combination of prescription medicine for up to six months along with some talk therapy.

I recently had a friend with severe OCD (obsessive-compulsive disorder). After having a couple difficult talks with him, he admitted there he needed help. First, he started counseling. Soon, he started on medication, and after a time, he felt better. So, he thought that he didn't need counseling anymore – because he felt better. But he was still doing many of the OCD activities that were a problem. He needed continued counseling to help him make changes to his behavior, which would be easier because he felt better.

Minor Distractions

There can be literally hundreds of minor distractions when you are discipling someone. I would like to address just two of them and let you decide how others might work themselves out.

Who doesn't have a smartphone today? Yes, I'm going there – that dreadful wireless monster that you can't function without. There seems to be an unconscious idea that every time your cell phone goes off, you absolutely must look at it. Instant messaging might be bad at work, but at least you can turn it off for a few hours of sleep. Many

---

[65] Medical Disclaimer: As a registered nurse, I do not prescribe any type of treatment or the length of treatment. But I am aware that most effective treatments last from six to twelve months.

people now sleep with their cell phones under their pillows to assess how well they sleep. Basically, with a medical reason to do that, it's just silly.

Yes, I come from a generation of corded phones. If the phone rang at dinner time, we simply ignored and continued with our family time. Then came answering machines, and now we have voicemail. But today, we rarely allow a call to go to voicemail. We instinctively look at our cell phone to see who's calling. Then we determine whether continuing our current conversation is as important as the person calling in. And it's not just incoming calls: text messages, social media notifications. And last night at dinner with friends, we each got an Amber Alert for something that was happening in North Texas (a five-hour drive away).

Two things happen when your cell phone dings, chirps, plays a part of a song, or whatever else you have it programmed to do. The first is that you tend to lose your train of thought. You're in the middle of an important point, and that little electronic demon (yes, I called it that) interrupts you. Once you're back, you're not really back yet. Studies have shown how each of these interruptions decreases your effectiveness.[66]

The second thing that happens is what goes on in the mind of the person you are with when you can't break away from your phone (be that a disciple or your family). What is being communicated, like it or not, is that whoever is calling or just tweeted is more important than they are. And over some time, this gets reinforced deeply into their souls. They simply aren't that important to you.

When I meet with someone, I usually either put my phone on silent or, better yet, turn it off. This sends a different message to the person in front of you; that they *are* the most important thing that is happening during that hour. I might need to turn it back on to schedule our next meeting. But that sends another message that the person is important enough to get it on my calendar right away.

IF, and that's a big if, you happen to be expecting an important call, the best thing you can do is ask if it's okay to leave your phone on to receive it. I've never had anyone say "no." It again lets the emerging disciple know that our meeting together is important.

---

[66] I have been significantly influenced by Cal Newport's book, *Deep Work: Rules for Focused Success in a Distracted World* (2016). I learned so much that I turned it back in to the public library and bought my own copy!

Now for that second minor distraction. Anyone who meets with me knows that when my phone is off, I usually have a small field notebook with me to jot down some key thoughts or prayer needs. Sometimes I just write on a paper napkin! After the meeting, I will transfer notes about the meeting and any follow-up that I need to do on a phone app – after the meeting, not at the end.

Having been a nurse in a hospital for many years, I know that things aren't done until the nurse's note was written. More importantly, by writing things down and then reviewing the notes before my next meeting, I didn't forget important items.

Here's why I decided that was so valuable. I met with someone several years back who wanted me to disciple him. I was confused because I thought he was being discipled by another person. He was, but he wanted a change.

As he told the story, every time he met with the other person, he would be asked how his parents were. His mother died at least seven years before this time. After telling the leader four times that his mother was no longer living, he felt that the leader didn't care enough to remember one of the most important things that ever happened to him. I could see the angst in his eyes as he told the story.

In order not to make the same mistake, I started making notes. It was really helpful for me at the time. I was discipling a couple guys who had lost their mothers; others had lost their fathers, and one father was an alcoholic and another severely impaired with major depression. There was no way I was going to keep all those family pieces correct, so I *had* to write them down.

Reviewing your notes before a meeting, even if it's the morning before an evening meeting, can work wonders. You can then check on how recent events turned out. Ask if there was an answer to a prayer request. You can even do a short review of the last topic you covered and whether there are any additional thoughts since your last meeting. All these follow-up steps from notes will indicate that the person in front of you is important. And that bonds you more deeply.

There are other distractions that I could cover. The simplest thing to do, though, is to think about what distractions occurred in the last two meetings you had. Once you identify them – they were there – you can think through how to cut the ones that can have the most impact. As I think about my meetings, I'm reminded that I need to start sitting with my back to the people traffic. I'm a people watcher, and if I watch every person who goes by, I communicate that the person in front of me is less important than a total stranger. Ouch!

There are plenty of books that help you make connections and communicate with good body language. Pick one and develop that part of your personal style. It will pay off because your disciple will feel more bonded to you and trust you more.

Distractions are part of life. They should be more like speed bumps than walls that we need to hurdle—although walls may go up when we least expect them. Being aware that distractions are normal will help us see them when they present themselves. Maintaining our values of being disciples who make disciples can help us overcome some distractions.

CHAPTER 37

Should I Always Be Discipling Someone?

Is this a rhetorical question? One that expects a certain reply? How can you even ask someone who has given his entire adult life to making disciples this question? Okay, I'm teasing; maybe a little.

The keyword in this question is "always." It has a broad meaning. It could even mean "in your sleep." It was one of my wife's favorite words. "You always do that." "Always?" I would ask. "Well, maybe not in your sleep," she would reply, "but I can't be sure."

"Always" might mean that there is someone that you can currently point to that you are discipling. Knowing the man who sent me an email asking this very question, I understand what he means.

Dawson Trotman (1906-1956) was the founder of The Navigators, a disciple-making ministry. He could be called the father of the modern disciple-making movement. Like how William Carey was the father of the modern missionary movement.

While I never met Dawson, I have known men who not only met him, some even lived in his home. Dawson asked one question more than any other: "Where's your man?" You might say Dawson's question was also rhetorical. He expected a certain answer. He wanted to hear about the man you were currently discipling.[67]

I think a better way to phrase this question would be, "Is there a time when I may not be discipling someone?" (Dawson would

---

[67] You can listen to Dawson Trotman ask this very question in a message entitled "Born to Reproduce." Find it on the Discipleship Library website at: http://www.discipleshiplibrary.com/dawson_trotman.php

probably say, "Yes. When you're dead!") But it is a legitimate question that begs a reasonable answer.

A disciple-making champion, LeRoy Eims, spoke about reasons that someone did not reproduce. He pointed to three main things that kept someone from discipling: immaturity, illness, or lack of contact. LeRoy compared it to someone trying to have a baby. He can't have a baby if he isn't mature. An illness might cause him to be sterile. Or he just wasn't "with" someone (we can't do it alone!).

LeRoy's point was that an immature faith prevents discipling. Sin (spiritual illness) prevents production. And not being around younger believers prevents reproduction.

If any of these three "symptoms" apply to you, I suggest doing something about that symptom. If there some sin that holds you back, remove it (Hebrews 12:1)! Do you feel immature, build your life on Christ (Colossians 2:7)! Are you in a place where you're not rubbing elbows with others, move! Or at least get out of that rut![68]

There are times when you may not disciple someone. People know that I tell newlyweds to focus on developing their relationship. Discipling others can rest for a time; perhaps a year. The Old Testament Law directed newly married men to stay off the battlefield for one year.

There's a time for a sabbatical, even for laymen. A friend of mine had been discipling guys and leading a small group for eight years. Some things began to happen with one of his children. For a time, it was more important to put more effort into his home, especially his son. I asked him to put discipling on hold. Follow Paul's counsel in 1 Timothy 3:5. Put a priority on your own household before diving into more ministry.

When my wife began to fight breast cancer, my ministry had to slow down. When a project in my corporate job required long hours for a couple months, ministry had to slow down. My point is that there are times when our discipling should decrease or even go on hold. The challenge is that we need to get back to it once things are back to normal.

One specific thought about family. There will always be challenges in your marriage, children, as well as your job. We need to make sure we don't use our family as an excuse not to disciple someone else. Let your disciple know about your challenges. Let him

____

[68] My old (deceased) friend, John Crawford, used to say that a rut was nothing more than a grave with the ends kicked out. So get out of that grave!

see how you apply God's Word to the situation. Let him hear how you pray over your family. By doing these things, you'll be building a stronger disciple.

I have had some Christian men tell me that they are discipling their children. That was their focus, and the "reason" they were not discipling a man. I asked a fellow what he was doing with his children. Monday evening was Taekwondo. Tuesday soccer practice. Wednesday was AWANAs (a children's church ministry). Thursday was gymnastics. Friday was Boy Scouts. Saturday afternoon was a soccer game. (I get tired just writing all of that!) But my question to him was, "When do you actually disciple them?"

I understand how there is no time to disciple someone when we have our kids in an activity every day of the week. Let's not fool ourselves. Very few of these activities, if any, result in a child becoming a disciple. We have plenty of children raised in this pattern who have left the Church when they leave their parent's homes.

In the meantime, there's a man who needs someone to invest an hour into his life. And he's neglected for the sake of your kids being "well-rounded." It doesn't take much to realize that if this man isn't helped, his family is also not helped. And people he works with don't have a godly man who can stand for Christ in the workplace. Or his neighborhood. There's no impact. Anywhere!

Oh, what God can do with one man who is wholly devoted to him and his Great Commission. And, oh, what's not done when we step out of the battle or ever enter the battle at all.

Another one of my mentors asked me what I am giving my life to. He would then ask me to fit each of my activities into one of the categories of building materials found in 1 Corinthians 3:12:

"Now if any man builds on the foundation with gold, silver, precious stones, wood, hay, straw" (NASB).

He reminded me that the wood, hay, and straw items will someday be burned up. The gold silver and precious stones would last, and even be refined. He would ask, "Are you giving your life to things that will rust, rot, and burn?" (He also used James 5:1-3 when he talked about this with me.)

One of the guys I mentor has had a series of moves and job changes. Just this morning, we talked about who he was discipling. No one was on the radar. He had done well discipling a guy from church in another city. But there wasn't anyone currently. He felt like he was in a situation that required plowing a field before he could plant the gospel.

I shared some thoughts from Isaiah 28:23-24:

> Listen and hear my voice;
>
> pay attention and hear what I say.
>
> When a farmer plows for planting, does he plow continually?
>
> Does he keep on breaking up and working the soil?

This verse shows that there *is* a certain time to plow and then to plant. In later verses from this chapter of Isaiah, God will talk about when and how to thresh the harvest. My point was that farming involves seasons; doing certain things at certain times. There are times to plow, plant, water, and wait for the harvest.

In the same way, there are seasons involved in making disciples. Our disciple-making season runs from a figurative spring to fall, just like the farming seasons. A season comes when we can rest. But if that season lasts more than a few months, we might be in the wrong place. Or looking for the wrong thing.

CHAPTER 38

Is It Okay to Take a Break? If So, How Long?

This question is like the last one I answered about "always" discipling someone. I believe there are valid reasons to take a break. So, the question is valid. However, I will specify upfront that a break should probably not last more than a year.

I mentioned before someone being in a new marriage. The Old Testament forbids a man to go to war for one year after his marriage. The reason was so he could have a child with his wife. There may have been another reason as well. A newly married man has things on his mind that can distract him from the battle.

These might be minor distractions (see chapter 36). There were times when I wrote letters and poems to my new wife when I should have been taking care of my military equipment. (The American military has no rule against sending newly married men away from their wives.) The distractions could also be major, like daydreaming instead of watching for the enemy.

Discipling can be hard. Some fellows can take more emotional energy from us. Sometimes it takes more than what we think we have to give. As a discipling relationship with someone like this comes to an end, it might be time for a break. You can give extra time to your family or take time to refresh yourself. Even when you are discipling someone, it's a good idea to have mini-breaks. Maybe a weekend away, and a week or two of vacation. He'll survive without you!

My wife was good at letting me know when I needed to take one of these breaks. There were projects that I need to do – sometimes with her. Or she was just looking for some extra time. (Every married man should have a date night on the calendar, especially when discipling someone else.)

Here's a caution, though. The maturity level of your wife can affect how much you can disciple. If your wife is looking for you to meet every one of her needs, there's a problem. You'll never be able to meet all of them. No matter what. If an area of insecurity pops up, discipling less only covers up the insecurity. Men need to know their wives well. That's a major reason for a date night, where we don't just watch a movie, but learn about each other deeply and help each other grow.

When my wife and I were going through premarital counseling, the chaplain gave us a personality assessment. The results showed I maxed out the score in the social-active section. My soon-to-be wife got the lowest score in the same area the chaplain had ever seen. It revealed that what she wanted was for me to be home with her constantly. While I wanted to be out with people. We were indeed the opposite regarding introversion and extroversion.

The solution was not to stay home and sit on the sofa every night. It was to find a balance between the two of us. I needed to give her ample time, but she needed to allow me to be with the guys. It was hard for both of us. Yet over time, we adapted. We even took a second one of those tests and found that we were growing closer together in that area!

Taking a break to address these pertinent areas may be the best thing you can do to be a lifelong disciple-maker, and to stay married! Ignoring these areas can even take you out of the race permanently. Having someone who is mentoring you is extremely helpful in these situations.

Yes, there will be times when we need to take a break from discipling someone for a time. If that "time" lasts too long, we need to re-evaluate what we're doing. Or what God is trying to do in our lives that is taking so long.

CHAPTER 39

What Do I Need to Cover to Disciple Someone?

Before we get into specifics, let me say this first. Anything that you do when discipling needs to contribute directly to someone growing in the traits of a disciple. There is much more than his biblical knowledge in view as you disciple him.

I began to meet with a man who was rough around the edges. That was to be expected because he had been around others just like him in the military. But he wasn't in the military anymore. How he was around nothing but civilians. They didn't understand that roughness that he had come to faith around.

As I began to develop a relationship with him, I first accepted him for who he was. But once that relationship was solid, I talked about those rough edges. And one of the things I asked him to do was read Dale Carnegie's book *How to Win Friends and Influence People*. More than anything else, this was the most impactful contribution I had on him.

I bring this up first because we often limit making disciples to getting them baptized and taught (Matthew 28:19-20). If your disciple is so obnoxious that no one wants to be around him, you won't be making a disciple who can make other disciples. Unless they are as equally obnoxious as him!

When this question was first posed to me, it included a couple specifics: "Read the Word? Spend time together?" Yes, to both of those!

We shouldn't just talk about the Bible; we should be in it together. When I first became a Christian, my disciple-maker had to teach me how to use my Bible. I had been raised in a church. The pastor would often say, "The Bible says..." (Just like Billy Graham did!) But I didn't know how to see what the bible actually said. I just took the pastor's word for it.

Where do you need to start with your disciple? Do you need to show him where to read? Just like this book, we have options on where to start. We can jump around. We don't have to get bogged down in the Old Testament law. We can start with Jesus (the Gospels) and work our way through.

You might need to talk about what a devotional life looks like. How can your disciple have a "quiet time"? How do you make sure he understands the difference between simply being quiet and having a devotional? Should he start with a printed devotional, like *Our Daily Bread* or *The Upper Room*? (My grandmother used these until she died.)

Do you need to have a quiet time with him? My disciple-maker met with me, and we would read through a Bible passage. We would reflect on that and pray together about what we learned. That helped me immensely to understand how to have my devotions.

Discipling someone means more than checking to see if he's been doing it. It's asking him what God has been saying. Asking him how he's being affected by that. But just as important is that you share what you've been getting yourself. Your sharing sets a pattern for him; of what to look for in devotional times and how to teach someone else!

All of this requires that you spend time with him. But that's intentional time *and* unintentional time. You need to plan to teach him about quiet times and have quiet times together. But you also need to have fun together. It's amazing how much you can learn about someone playing putt-putt golf or ultimate Frisbee. Even going to a movie can give you the chance to talk about something you noticed in the show.

I once was able to watch a guy I was meeting with "do evangelism" at his dorms. One of the guys from his wing was doing some car repairs. My disciple was standing nearby, talking. Not helping; just talking.

What did I do? I invited my disciple over to help me change the oil. He stood and watched me. I asked him to get under the chassis to help. He resisted. That gave me the chance to talk about how important it is to connect with a project. If we can't make that connection, it can hinder our relationships.

Please do spend time together. Time to disciple in his faith, time to develop as a person, and time to develop a closer bond.

I do not intend to endorse any disciple-making materials. Most materials, by the way, are sold under the term "discipleship" rather than disciple-making. Another possible term that is still used today is "spiritual formation." That means as you look at things on discipleship, it may take a while to find things to help you make disciples.

Instead, I want to point back to the first question in this section about what a disciple *is*, and work from there. Those of us who have been making disciples for a while, often refer to what we teach as "the basics." These are the things that, at a minimum, identify what a disciple is and does.

These include a relationship with Jesus Christ that gets deeper over time. This is reflected by submitting to His lordship and obeying Him; two traits that set true disciples apart from believers. There are at least four things that help a believer grow here: time in the Word and prayer, fellowship with other believers, and some type of a witness.

Discipling goes beyond those "basics." It begins to touch on the character of the person. It looks at how that walk with Christ affects his job performance. He won't be able to witness to co-workers if his attitude stinks. We tend to jump into the area of witnessing too early.

That doesn't mean that someone shouldn't share their testimony with a co-worker. But if their work ethic hasn't changed yet, sharing testimonies can fall on deaf ears. Your disciple needs to win the abililty to share with someone; not just slam them like a wrecking ball. Nobody likes getting hit by one of those.

You also need to make sure that your emerging disciple is making connections with other Christians. And sometimes, we need to caution against certain Christians. I have a guy I mentor who works with other Christians. They believe they are now perfect and cannot sin. I had to address this idea to help him understand his biblical position in Christ.

Another area to address is family matters. Oh, my goodness, have I gotten into heavy talks about things. When meeting in public, we had to use code words or letters not to be heard by those around us. How is he doing with the kids? How is he loving his wife and only her? These are areas that disciples must be improving in. I won't go into those private conversations here.

We can't just ask our disciples about their family matters. We need to observe them ourselves. (There's more of that idea of spending time together.) One man I've been mentoring told me about the problems he was having with one of his kids. I made sure to watch their interaction the next chance I got.

He was having problems. And he was initiating some of them. As soon as we had time to talk in private, I gave him clear examples of his actions and the child's response. He was made at her response but had not considered his cause of the conflict. It was an area that we would work on for several months afterward. And I continued to observe.

With all that I've said above, you might begin to understand why I suggest you only disciple one or two men at a time. And most of what I've talked about above is not included in current discipleship materials. There is no book designed to meet the needs of each man you disciple. It takes thought, prayer, and effort. Along with a humble approach.

Sometimes sticking to knowing the Bible is easier. But if we are going to make a disciple who can make more disciples, it will be work for you. It sure won't be easy!

Making This Yours

Reflect back on how you were discipled (assuming that you had a disciple-maker investing in your life). What were the things that your disciple-maker did well? What could he have done better? What topics were most helpful? Were there topics that didn't hit the mark?

After thinking about these things, how can you do something similar in another person's life?

CHAPTER 40

How Many Men Can I Disciple at Once, and Do it Well?

My answer is going to be based on a guess. My guess is that this question comes from someone married with children, and he works in a full-time job. That covers most men and many women. Remove any of these variables, and my suggested amount might go higher. Might.

My answer is also based on discipling another person through a one-on-one meeting; not how many people should be in a small group.

I mentor and coach many guys in this phase of life. Demands are not only in the home and workplace. The local church looks for them to be involved. Life groups and Bible studies take one evening from the week and can often require preparation. There can also be weekly financial management classes, serving in the parking lot or Sunday children's program.

With a load anything like this, I will advise you to not disciple more than two people at the same time. That would be on either a weekly or every other week schedule. Often though, my answer may be only one at a time. ("At a time" doesn't refer to the one-to-one meeting, but to only meeting regularly with one man. Just to be clear!)

Let's take my advice of no more than two and cut it in half. Change to goal to disciple just one person at any one time. My friend Mel does just that. He has a full-time job, a wife, and eight children. He disciples one person over three to five years. But he does it consistently. For the past 20 years, he has focused on one man at a time.

Let's say that it takes Mel four years to fully disciple a man who can then disciple another. Assume the guy is around for a full four years. In twenty years, Mel would have (and has) discipled five men. Each of those men can disciple other men. So, Mel doubles his output every four years, from one guy to two, to four, to eight, to sixteen. At the end of 20 years there will be 32 disciples who can disciple others. All from one man focusing on one disciple at a time.

Before I go further, let me cast a vision. What would happen if every Christian was discipling one other person? Either men-to-man or ma'am to ma'am? If you are in a small group, you may know at least nine others. You plus nine others can result in ten other people being discipled.

Take it one more step. How many small groups are there in your church? Let's guess that there might be four. Four groups of ten people would be 40 people discipling 40 others. "No man is an island" (so the saying goes).

The point is there are plenty of people who can be making disciples. (Not that they are right now. Just that they can.) You won't be the *only* disciple-maker out there. There's no need to ignore your family. No need to be lackluster at work. You might feel the need to disciple ten people all by yourself. But you won't do it well. Discipling one or two is enough.

Now, let's come back to the original number: two. That's a reasonable number. Unless you're just starting out. Then maybe you want to stick with one for your first go at it.

What you need to do, whether it is two or just one, is to look at your schedule. Find some openings. Don't neglect early morning or lunchtime. Most of us commute to work. There's almost always a place to meet along the way. And most of us get a lunch period. These are great times to meet with someone. Granted, in this situation, time is short. Both of you need to get back to work.

Meetings do not need to take two hours to be effective. (We all know the longer the meeting, the less useful it can be.) You can meet for 30 minutes and be effective; if you plan your time. Many of us can, in fact, carve two one-hour blocks of time out of our schedules. That gives you enough bandwidth to disciple two men.

Before you think you can handle more than two, I would caution you. Discipling someone well takes more than a one-hour block of time (a combination of meeting and traveling back and forth). You need time to review what you talked about on your last visit. Take time to plan what to talk about next. Take time to pray during the week (not just at the meeting). Remember how much Paul wrote that he was praying for people? I would say that one one-hour block of meeting time requires at least another hour of prep and prayer. But that gets into another question.

If you're new to discipling someone, start with one. As you hone your skills, add another. Just be careful if you're tempted to add a third. While your skilled do become honed, and the topics become familiar, your presentation will change with each man – because there's no cookie-cutter method that's effective for everyone.

If you are a college student, or not married or retired, you may have more time. However, I will still exhort you to make sure you think beyond the one-hour meeting. I find the more guys I meet with, the more I need to plan and pray. Nothing's worse than talking about the same thing because you forgot where you were from week to week.

Side note: I keep a record of what we talk about with every meeting. I currently use an app of my cell phone called Google Keep. A friend of mine uses Evernote. There's no one best app that I would recommend. But I would recommend keeping some notes – and reviewing them before your next meeting.

One other thing to think about, especially for those of us at or beyond retirement age. Part of discipling is keeping up with "trends." Many of the men I disciple are in their 20s and 30s. As I write this, that means they are Millennials and Gen Z. I need to stay abreast of these groups. Nothing is worse than not knowing what the current trends are that your emerging disciple* may be interested in.

I was stretched in my thinking on this idea at a meeting at Wheaton College. Someone named popular people, many of them Christians. These people were who emerging adults were listening to the most. I was vaguely familiar with only one of them. I decided I needed to do better.

There is also ongoing research on how these age groups think and feel. I need to understand what they value. How they respond to authority. Reading and incorporating this should be included in your discipling preparation time. It *will* make you a better disciple-maker.

One final thought. Leading a small group does not count as discipling. I'm pretty sure I've written this before. In small groups, people share ideas and encourage one another. But, each person (who is willing) needs some one-on-one time. It helps him process how to carry out spiritual disciplines and overcome barriers. See Question 30 for more about this.

Master plumbers don't train novice plumbers in a classroom. They get down under the sink and show them how to do the work. People may get some emotional help from support groups. But personal counseling needs to be behind closed doors to address deep issues. And so does discipling others. It doesn't take a personal office, den, or study—a coffeehouse will suffice—but it *is* highly personal time done best one-to-one.

Start discipling one person and do it well. Work your way to two as your methods and modeling improve. Want more than two? Ask your wife first. If she's in agreement, take a third. If not, love your wife. You made a lifelong commitment to her. Honor it!

How Do I Tell Someone that I Cannot Disciple Them?

That's a tough question. I'll answer from four perspectives: your schedule and abilities, and his schedule and abilities. These four areas are probably one of the main reasons behind not discipling someone.

As I mentioned in Question 40, I advise that men with home and work duties to disciple no more than two men. So perhaps you already have two men, and a third one approaches you. Don't be surprised when that happens. The guys you are investing in will mention it to others. Someone may notice how they are growing and ask what's going on. Or, your disciple may mention something he learned from you. Your name and role pique interest in men who want to grow deeply.

First, let's talk about the limits of your schedule. I had a "worst-case scenario" a few years ago. A pastor at my church mentioned during the sermon how I was investing in younger men. He had already asked me if it was okay to do that. But I didn't know he would point me out; "The guy in a red shirt; with a beard." At the end of the service, I was approached by nine men who wanted to meet with me. Even as a full-time disciple-maker, there was no way I could add that many guys! But I didn't say no to any of them. Uh?

In that case, I asked each of them to schedule some time with me. I pulled out my cell phone and went to my calendar. Anyone who sees my online calendar sees red and blue blocks already filling the days.

(Red is for ministry meetings. Blue is for home duties – like putting out the trash. Yes, that's on my calendar, too!)

Some men who saw my calendar may quickly said that it looks like I'm too busy for them. Perhaps it's just that they don't see a time that's convenient for them. Three of the nine guys asking took themselves out of the running. Perhaps they weren't as hungry as they needed to be yet.

I did schedule meetings with the other six men. As I put those meetings into my calendar, I also handed them a small booklet (I carry a few) and asked them to read it before we met. Believe it or not, three of them said they were too busy to read it! I let them know when they can read it, I would be happy to meet with them after that. Those meetings were removed from my calendar. This was more about the limits of their schedules than mine. They're probably not *that* busy. They just don't want something bad enough to make room.

Three men did take the booklets and committed to reading them before our meeting. I learned at our meetings that two of them didn't get around to reading. I didn't just write them off. I asked them to let me know when they had read the booklet, and then we could meet up. (They never did.) In the meantime, I would pray for each man. One did read it. I am still meeting with that one man.

This story reminds me of Jesus healing the ten lepers. Only one returned to thank him (Luke 17:11-19). The "dropout rate" seems to be about the same.

Likewise, someone may want to meet, but he doesn't have the time himself. This can be for several reasons. I knew one fellow who was trying to get his financial service business off the ground. He usually made it to church, but little else. A building contractor was only able to meet during bad weather – that's hard to plan out in advance!

When a guy can't find time in his schedule, let him know you can meet when his calendar has some room in it. You could suggest a time management course through the church or another source. Don't just leave the guy hanging. Try to give him some options.

But when it comes to someone else's schedule, you may find yourself fighting against Parkinson's Law. That principle says, "Work expands to fill the time available for its completion." In this context, what it means is that people allow all the "stuff" of life to fill up their schedule, and then they find it very difficult to cut urgent things away to make room for important things.[69]

A third reason to not disciple a guy is when you don't feel qualified to help the fellow. Perhaps you feel like he's further along than you are. Maybe there are some special needs that he has. You just don't feel like you can help.

There is one area where this comes through most: if you have never been married, but he is. Most single guys just don't get all the concerns of a married man. Single guys may be limited to helping other single guys. However, a married man can help both married and single men. And don't let me leave out two other groups of men: widowers and divorced men. Even these men can teach others the basics of being a disciple.

This difference isn't always a barrier. Perhaps a married guy wants to learn how to have a quiet time, and that's one of your strengths. There's no reason that, as a single guy, you can't help him with that. But when it comes to matters in the home, a single guy is better off letting another married man take that on. (Refer to Question 14 in Section One about working together as a disciple-making team for more about this idea.)

The next reason (his abilities) can be a tough one. We often allow ourselves to experience a guilt trip. We're supposed to love everyone, especially other believers. So, we might want to lower our standards and give the guy a pass. Don't do that!

Here are a couple things that have happened to me recently. One guy didn't really want to be discipled. He wanted to talk about his marriage problems. Helping someone with marriage problems is NOT discipling. And you're probably not qualified to give marriage counseling. Someone else isn't being discipled because you're trying to counsel the wrong man.

Another guy was having periods of depression. He wanted a friend. I like being friends, but not when it takes away from obeying Christ's command to make disciples. While I am a registered nurse, I am not a therapist, nor can I prescribe medicines. Helping him would mean that another guy isn't being discipled.

---

[69] May I suggest a small booklet at this point? Charles Hummel wrote a little pamphlet in the 1960s entitled *Tyranny of the Urgent*. You can find print version of it to buy, or electronic versions available for free online. It's one of the booklets that I carry to ask someone to read when we first schedule a meeting.

While these are real problems that we will come across, most guys just don't meet the criteria we are looking for (see Chapter 8 in Section One about the minimum needs of a man to disciple).

So, while we do not want to take on a guy that doesn't have the qualities we're looking for, we can give some hope. Tell him that you're looking for a certain type of guy to invest in. Give him the criteria. Line it out for him. You'll be surprised how many guys will come back and tell you that they did work on the criteria and are ready to meet.

When you decide that you cannot help a man consider pointing him in a direction where he can get help. If a guy is asking for help, help him find it. If he's struggling with a sin that you're not comfortable addressing, point him to someone who can. Whatever his needs help him make a connection. Introduce him to someone you know can help him. Tell him you'll even make some calls to locate somebody.

Eventually, as you point out these qualities and needs in a man's life, you can help prepare him to become a disciple who makes disciples.

CHAPTER 42

What's the Difference between Discipling and Mentoring?

People who know me well become aware that I use these two words quite differently. Not everyone does. I have found that Millennials and Gen Zs use the term mentoring as a catch-all term. Whether in regards to their family, faith, work, or personality; it's all mentoring to them. Yet there is a difference in my mind. Let me explain.

Discipling is teaching the basics* of the Christian life. I'll use a basketball analogy to describe what I mean. The San Antonio Spurs is a professional basketball team that is coached by Greg Popovich. He played himself at the U.S. Air Force Academy for four years. He knows how to play the game. He often teaches children the basics of the game. This is a form of discipling.

Mentoring takes people who know the basics to another level – the level of a mentor. Popovich has mentored NBA players who became coaches like him.[70] The modern use of the word mentoring comes from the business world. Someone in leadership looks for a subordinate in his organization or even outside the organization. The mentor then helps that person move up the ladder to a position like his own. My pastor does something very similar—helping a few

---

[70] Avery Johnson and Steve Kerr come to mind immediately.

Christians in our church develop as pastors themselves and helping a few young pastors outside the church become better pastors.

A third term that is used is coaching; which Popovich is currently doing. As a coach, Popovich helps men who are better ballplayers than he is. He isn't mentoring them; they're already better than him at playing, and they don't want to become a coach (at least not yet). But Popovich looks within them—or helps them look within themselves—to become even better players than they are, or he could ever hope to be.

Jesus told us to make disciples. As we've seen in Question 17, those disciples then making other disciples is implied in the Great Commission. Most of our work will be done in making disciples; discipling others in the basics. I've already alluded to the fact that most people won't be in the same location for more than five years. So, we have the opportunity to make a lot of disciples!

Along the way, we will find disciples who need help making disciples. This can be mentoring a disciple to begin to make other disciples (a term the Bible uses is equipping). Our job here is to remind them of the spiritual basics that they already possess. Then help them figure out how to help others do that, as well. We may ask them to join us in a discipling meeting we have with someone. We may give them some tools and show them how to use them. Our objective is to mentor them to be disciple-makers like us.

The word in the Bible that comes closest to the idea of mentoring is *equipping*. Paul wrote that God gave the Church certain roles to equip the saints for the work of the ministry (Ephesians 4:11-12). Other verbs are also used, such as to "complete" or "perfect." To equip someone for ministry, some basics need to be there already. You're building on what's already there.

Our focus in this book is discipling. Yet, we need to be aware that there is more involved for some. You may mentor some; you may coach some. But be discipling is the central focus for every mature member of the Body of Christ.

I feel the need to insert a word of caution here. There are many young Christians who emotionally struggle. It's quite easy in a discipling or mentoring relationship for these issues to come up. They sure do with some fellows that I have met with in the past.

As believers, we need to encourage one another (1 Thessalonians 5:11). That might include some "light" counseling. We need to know, though, when someone needs help beyond what we can give.

Discipling might include some biblical counseling, but it should not be obscured by emotional needs.

Discipling definitely includes asking how things are going and giving encouragement. I do this a lot. When I hear the deeper issues come up, I ask, "What did your counselor say about that?" If the counselor or pastor is addressing it, I encourage that person to keep talking with the counselor. If they haven't brought it up, I encourage them to do that on the next visit.

One person I began to meet with had clear signs of major depression.[71] I pressed this guy to seek a counselor. He did. As part of the therapy, the counselor asked him to only meet with his counselor and his pastor. The counselor felt three people focusing on three areas weren't helpful. I agreed and stepped aside. We need to do what's best for each man and not let our partialities get in the way.

There's an old saying – "too many cooks spoil the broth." Someone who needs counseling only needs one person helping their emotional health. When the problem is resolved or manageable, you can pick discipling back up then. You might need to refresh a few topics, but it'll be fine.

Here's one more tidbit. When I was newly married, my wife became pregnant. We told everyone about the good news. But two months later, she lost the baby. We were crushed. As people learned about that, they seemed to feel that they *had* to say something. In every case, what they said was not helpful and even sometimes hurtful. They meant well, like Job's friends. But sometimes the best thing we can do is just love someone without trying to cap it off with a Bible verse. If the man you disciple is going through hard times, don't say much of anything. Be present. Your love and presence will say plenty.

Do look for opportunities to disciple, mentor, and coach others. But stick to what you know. If you don't know, hold your tongue. We may be well-meaning, but it can still hurt.

Disciple well. Mentor well. Coach well. Listen for, "Well done."

---

[71] As a licensed registered nurse, I can detect and observe signs and symptoms of mental health problems. I cannot diagnosis or treat them. You shouldn't try either.

CHAPTER 43

Is There Anything that Should be Avoided when Discipling?

This might be the best question I've addressed in this book. YES! Several things should be avoided when discipling others. The very first thing that I would caution against is discipling someone of the opposite sex. Call it the influence of Billy Graham or Vice President Pence. Trouble can always be brewing beneath the surface when you meet with someone of the opposite sex.

I am aware that professional counselors must provide privacy so their opposite sex clients can speak freely. However, you're probably not a professional counselor. (If you are, you already know of the dangers that lurk behind the closed door.) I have a good friend whose father was a military chaplain. As such, he was counseling military wife from the chapel who was having marital problems. Things did not go as they should have. The result was the two of them divorcing their spouses and marrying one another. While this example might be extreme, it's not unusual. Unfortunately.

One of the things that I have grown to appreciate is that men and women disciple each other differently. It's one of those Venus-and-Mars situations. No matter what the secular world may say, men and women *do* communicate differently. That can work its way out in how they follow Jesus and grow in communion with him. If you can't understand how your wife thinks or feels, how can you hope to disciple some other woman? Really, just don't.

We should only meet one-on-one with someone of the opposite sex (other than our spouse) under rare circumstances. Most pastors that I know will leave their office door open when talking with a woman. And as a secondary precaution, the church secretary is on duty right outside the office door during the meeting time.

When you disciple someone, you're probably not meeting in an office. You may think that a public area, like a coffee shop, is a safe place. Because you've never seen anyone being intimate in a public space. (Maybe you need to get out more!) But it's a risk you should not attempt to take.

The greatest difficulty arises when you become aware of someone of the opposite sex who wants to be discipled but can't find a disciple-maker. This can often happen when a man disciples another man, and his wife wants to "get what he's been getting." I understand a wife wanting something that no one is providing, but you're simply *not* the answer to her dilemma.

There are a few (statistically speaking) married couples who are both able to disciple others. Often, they will each meet one-on-one with the same-sex person and occasionally meet as two couples to address any "couple" issues. I've known a few couples who meet with another couple in their home together, then split into different rooms in the house to talk man-to-man and ma'am-to-ma'am. These are best-case scenarios, but may not represent your situation, especially if you have led a co-worker to Christ whose spouse has not become a believer yet.

There has only been one time in my life when I agreed to meet with a young single woman. She was in the military, and she knew several of the men I was discipling. She wanted the same help I was giving to others. She searched for a woman to help her but couldn't find one. I only agreed on special circumstances. I rearranged my meetings with two other military men and gave her the slot in between.

We met in a fast-food restaurant. She would arrive while I was finishing with one man, and when the second man arrived, it was time for her to leave. And, most importantly, my wife knew where I was and who I was with. She agreed to the arrangement for a *limited* time. My wife had three small children and simply could not travel across town to the military base to help the young lady. And it was a limited time – three, perhaps four, months.

If God is truly sovereign – and he is – we need to trust that he will provide for the discipling needs of opposite-sex people. We are not his gift to the Church to meet all these needs. And if it's not happening, God is still sovereign. Provide alternatives to one-on-one discipling: books, podcasts, Bible studies. Just don't try to do it yourself. It might work once, but it can get you later once your guard is down. Better safe than sorry.

There are a few other things I would caution you to avoid. The second is a god-complex, feeling that you can provide everything that someone "needs" in his life. If we're going to be good at discipling, we're probably going to be bad at something else. And even as disciple-makers, there will be certain topics that we will excel at and others where we need to improve ourselves. We simply can't meet every need of every person.

In my early days as a Christian, the man who discipled me wasn't all that much farther along than I was. Fortunately, we would attend large group meetings or conferences where there were other men farther along than both of us. He would point out someone in the crowd and say, "See that guy? Ask him to get a meal or to talk during the free time."

While I am slightly introverted, I always took him up on his advice. I would approach the stranger and introduce myself. He would show me his packed schedule but always had a space available. We would meet, and he would share earthquake-inducing thoughts from his Bible. I would always come away from these short, one-off meetings inspired and committed to growing more in whatever my newest friend talked with me about.

Little did I know that often my disciple-maker had already talked with that "spiritual giant." Many of these men were known for being really, really good at a particular area of their spiritual lives. When my prayer life needed a booster shot, I would be directed toward the man who had a deep and effective prayer life.

The point of this is to let you know that you don't have to meet every need of the person you're discipling. Do what you do best and orchestrate life events so that others can make investments in your man. Even today, I still make this a practice of pointing out a man to talk with. However, in the past few years, I find more young guys approaching me asking to get a meal or coffee.

Funny story that might be a bit of a sidetrack. A few years ago, two college students approached me at a disciple-making conference.

They introduced themselves to me and then said, "We were told to find an "old man" to get some time with." I loved at them kindly, at least I tried, and said, "That might not be the best way to start out our time together." I later found out that they were told by another disciple-maker to state the request exactly that way. He knew I get a kick out of their request.

A third area that I would avoid involves expecting too much of others. If I had it my way, every man I disciple would be the next disciple-making giant. But that just doesn't happen that often. In fact, I think it's rare. Personally, I think you may only have one or two "Timothys" or "Issacs" (that key man on whom everything rests) in your lifetime of discipling others.

Yes, my expectation is for every man to be the best he can be, a disciple-maker among disciple-makers! Yet, forty years of experience has taught me that many men will eventually smolder into a wisp of smoke rather than burn like Nebuchadnezzar's furnace. So, don't be surprised when one of your guys hits bottom, or settles for the status quo. That's not a reason to feel like a failure. You just stay faithful to the Great Commission. The final outcome is your faithfulness to making disciples—what you do, not what they do.

I can't count the number of guys who have settled for less than what they were gifted for and able to attain. Each time that this has happened, I tend to hit a little "poor-me" time. I'll be honest. You can pour a lot of your life into someone only to not get the results you hoped for. But I need to shake off the self-pity and get back to what Jesus called me to do. Otherwise, there could be two casualties instead of one.

There may be a time when that person who let you down comes back around. Sometimes, it takes time, even years, to process the value of being a disciple and making disciples. I've had guys who have come back. I've also had a couple of them bomb out a second time. Hold each person you disciple with an open hand.

This is where that maxim to "expect the best, prepare for the worst" comes in very handy. The Apostle Paul probably had great expectations for his co-worker Demas (Philemon 1:24). The Bible gives us glimpses of Demas being distracted by other things. It's not clear what his distraction was. It's possible that he got back in the saddle. But according to the last letter that Paul wrote, Demas dismounted a second time (2 Timothy 4:10). Even with that "failure,"

Paul could say, "I have fought the good fight, I have finished the race, I have kept the faith" (2 Timothy 4:7).

Stay in the battle, guys!

Section Three

The Local Church and Disciple-Making

When I first envisioned this book, I only planned on two sections. Soon, friends heard I was looking for questions. Questions began to come in about discipling and the local church. So, I decided to add a third section to speak to the role of the church.

Let me be very clear from the beginning of this section. I am committed to my local church. I am a member, and I attend every Sunday when in town. I try to find a church when I am traveling, as well.

I do not want to generalize about how churches disciple their people. Every church seems to have a different approach. I personally prefer to attend churches on a more conservative side of the spectrum, so I can only speak accurately from that view. But I have visited several more progressive churches. That would include the First Baptist Church of America (Providence, Rhode Island). The day I was there, they were bringing their firearms to be turned into "plowshares." So, my view of these progressive churches is limited by experience, yet I believe I have had my finger on their pulse.

I want to give real answers to these questions. To provide balance, I will include some short responses from personal friends I know who serve as pastors. The goal is to provide a broader perspective than I may have myself. So, following each of my answers will be a short comment from a pastor who works in a church.

And finally, my focus here is on church members. Perhaps you are not a member who contributes directly to a local church, but rather someone who occasionally attends as a consumer. In that case, there's something different I'd like to say to you. Join a church and begin to practice being part of the Body of Christ!

Pastoral Response Providers

Pierce Eaton is an Associate Pastor at a church in Texas. He has a Bachelor of Science in international business from Southwest Texas State University (2012) and a Master of Arts in Theology from Liberty Baptist Theological Seminary. He is currently working on a Master of Divinity from Liberty. He is married with one daughter and has been making disciples and serving the local church for seven years.

Eli Gardner pastors a church in Oklahoma. He served in the United States Marine Corps Reserve from 1999 through 2005, participating in the invasion of Iraq in 2003. He has a bachelor's in Philosophy and Religion from Mississippi State University (2007), a Master of Divinity from Southwestern Baptist Theological Seminary (2011), and a Master of Arts in Professional Development from Dallas Baptist University (2015). He is currently working on a Ph.D. in Biblical Studies with an emphasis in ministry at Midwestern Baptist Theological Seminary. He is married and has one son with another child on the way.

Sean Russell served in the United States Air Force as an enlisted man and now serves as a Chaplain Candidate in the U.S. Air Force Reserves. Between his military service, he served as the Pastor of College Ministry and was responsible for the spiritual development and resiliency of the college-age students across two church campuses in Texas. He has a Bachelor of Science from the University of Central Florida (2010) and a Master of Divinity from Liberty Baptist Theological Seminary (2017). He is married with one daughter.

CHAPTER 44

What is the Role of the Local Church in Making Disciples?

"When the pastor does for people
what God has called the people to do,
everyone gets hurt and God's mission is hindered."[72]
Ed Stetzer

There can be no argument that the church should be making disciples. Jesus gave the entire worldwide Church* the Great Commission to make disciples. That includes every local church – the local gathering of members of the universal Church. Yet, many churches talk more about discipleship than about making disciples. We saw earlier in the book that these words do not mean the same thing, although people may use them interchangeably.

You may hear about local churches making disciples outside the walls of the church.[73] However, there are still many people in a

---

[72] Ed Stetzer. "A Reproducible Lifestyle and the De-emphasis of Clergy Can Lead to Movement" on The Exchange. Accessed on October 5, 2019 at: https://www.christianitytoday.com/edstetzer/2019/september/gospel-movements-whats-our-role-even-as-god-does-work.html

[73] A pastor in Colorado, Frank Tillapaugh, wrote an entire book about being outside the church walls. A used copy of the book can still be found, entitled *Unleashing the Church: Getting People Out of the Fortress and into Ministry* (Regal Books, 1985).

church* who consider disciple-making to be the job of the pastor. There have been plenty of times when I've heard, "That's what we pay him for."

I wrote about different disciple-making activities in the *Making Disciples* Section. These were: large groups, small groups, and one-on-one. The local church is best known for its large group meetings. The congregation gathers, with some non-Christians in the mix, for teaching, prayer, communion, and fellowship (Acts 2:42). Along with that mainstay, many churches now also host small groups. All these contribute to making disciples.

Many churches talk about their concern for making disciples. They often emphasize a particular action from within the Great Commission. There may be a duty felt toward one of the participle verbs: go, baptize, or teach. Some even measure the success of the church based on one of these actions. Many Baptist churches track the number of baptisms each year? My home church tracks the number of missionaries sent out each year. This includes many short-term trips that last seven to ten days and are mostly evangelism focused. But how many churches track the number of disciples made?

Perhaps we have not understood the Great Commission and its language structure. Those three activities are part of disciple-making – the main action verb. Doing one of them alone misses the mark.

To stimulate your thinking, I will quote a few church mission statements that I found and let you decide.[74]

> "To proclaim the Gospel of Christ and the beliefs of the evangelical Christian faith, to maintain the worship of God, and to inspire in all persons a love for Christ, a passion for righteousness, and a consciousness of their duties to God and their fellow human beings" – Michigan
>
> "To carry the gospel, the sacraments, and God's love and fellowship to the unchurched, the alienated, and the excommunicated (the church's homeless)" – Florida
>
> "To grow together toward a God who knows us and can help us put all the pieces of this sometimes bizzare [sic] world into perspective" – Alaska
>
> "Helping people become passionate, devoted followers of Jesus Christ" – Colorado

---

[74] These mission statements were found on May 24, 2019 at: https://www.missionstatements.com/church_mission_statements.html

"To glorify God by knowing, applying, and proclaiming the life-changing Gospel of Jesus Christ" – Virginia

"Following Christ's example, we welcome all on a spiritual journey" – Washington

Notice that not one of the examples here mentioned "disciple" or even discipleship. A couple do mention following Christ. The Church was commissioned to make disciples. But it seems to be absent from their mission statements. While some of the marks of a disciple are included, each individual mark alone does not give a complete picture.

"Putting together the pieces." "Being on a spiritual journey." It's no wonder that some question if the local church has lost its commitment to the Great Commission. I'm not trying to be harsh. I seem to be pointing out the elephant in the room.

Words like discipleship can imply being together in groups and might include talking about Jesus or the Bible. We can assume this leads to fulfilling the Great Commission. But it doesn't. It just adds to the confusion. When we exchange words like "follower" for "disciple," we add even more confusion. And when people are confused, they don't know what to do.

Jesus told us to make disciples; not followers, or to put the pieces together, or to go on a journey. There were concrete things that he said about being a disciple. He said there were things that if we didn't do them, we could not be a disciple. He also pointed to things that prove we are his disciples. All other things can become distractions. Distractions prevent us from doing the main thing Jesus said we are to do.

Steve Addison helps put this in perspective. He expresses concern that the Western church is in a "missional fog." A fog clouded by good things, such as ecology, equality, justice, and peace. He warns:

"All these activities and causes have been classified as 'mission.' But these are not the core missionary task. Some may be the fruit of the gospel, but they are not the gospel itself."[75]

As the Church, our marching orders are still found in the Great Commission. When we allow something else to take its place, we risk decreasing the advancement of the Kingdom of God in our time.

A friend taught me that a group will always adjust to its lowest common denominator. That common thing becomes what we people

---

[75] Steve Addison. The Rise and Fall of Movements: A Roadmap for Leaders. (100Movements Publishing, 2019), location 453. Kindle edition.

know us for. Few churches are known for making disciples. Common denominators in churches can be teaching the Word, reaching the poor, working toward justice. These are all good things that have replaced the best thing. Yet, by focusing on the good instead of the better, we have replaced the multiplier with the denominator.

We can see all these good things, these fruits of the gospel, in the Bible. Jesus did many of them himself; bringing healing and hope and pointing out injustice throughout the land. Yet focusing on these good things will tend to overcome the Great Commission – the better thing – just like Martha did (Luke 10:38-42). The commission was to obey everything he commanded. We simply cannot put another teaching, no matter how beloved it is, at a higher priority at the expense of the Great Commission.

Let me get back to the question about the local church's role. Every church should have the Great Commission as its focal point. And the focal point of the Great Commission is making disciples.

The focus of the church should be on making disciples. The Apostle Paul puts it another way. God gave the church leadership to equip the saints (that's the laymen*) for the work of the ministry (Ephesians 4:11-12).

Paul adds that the result of this type of ministry is "the building up of the body of Christ; until we all attain to the unity of the faith, and of the knowledge of the Son of God, to a mature man, to the measure of the stature which belongs to the fullness of Christ" (Ephesians 4:12b-13, NASB). This is a good description of a group of disciples!

We might view the church as a place that equips disciples to serve outside the church walls. Or as a place that uses disciples to build the walls and interior to keep the church going. Church growth experts talk about how church plants start with the first view and slowly move to the second. It seems that all organizations, whether religious or secular, eventually focus on self-preservation. The result, at least for the church, is a significant decrease in outreach.

If your church has lost its disciple-making focus, don't leave that church! Find two or three others and cast the vision of disciple-making to them. A small group of disciple-makers can grow in your church. And that micro-movement can grow and reach others. Your church can equip disciples for ministry to your community - with your help!

Pastoral Responses

Pierce Eaton

The primary emphasis and goal of the local church should always be to make and grow disciples. Sadly, many churches in our day have been built around the lesser goals of cultural relevance, social justice, and community impact. These are good secondary goals of the local church, but they should not be the finish line for which we are striving. All local churches should make reaching the lost with the gospel, teaching new believers, and raising disciples who make disciples their primary emphasis and goal. If a local church has the proper emphasis on discipleship and disciple-making, then that church will grow spiritually and numerically and will often attain its secondary goals in the end.

To best understand the role of the local church in disciple-making, I think it is good first to understand what the local church is. My simple definition of the local church: The local church is a group of believers who submit themselves under the authority of a pastor and elders, who regularly gather for corporate worship, and who are trained and taught by their church leaders so that they might be equipped to do ministry within and outside of their local church. Did you notice that my definition includes training and teaching? Training and teaching the church is the role of the pastor and church leaders, and the local church's role, as Bruce established, is to make disciples. This doesn't mean that the pastor does not make disciples, of course he does. However, his role (one of his many roles) within the local church is to teach and equip believers to become disciples who make disciples and to oversee the methods that the church utilizes in bringing about a discipling culture.

The disciples within the local church have a duty both inside and outside of their church. For a discipling culture to grow within a local church, the disciple-makers of that church must take it upon themselves to disciple other believers in their church. These same disciple-makers should also make efforts in disciple-making outside of their church. In other words, discipleship and evangelism go hand in hand. Disciple-making is the most effective evangelistic tool that the local church has, and it also is the most effective way of building up and teaching believers so that they become disciples who make disciples.

On a practical level, all disciples should be involved in a local church. The church plays a vital role in the life of the disciple and in their disciple-making. It further trains and equips them for disciple-making, gives them other disciples to learn from and lean on, and allows them the opportunity to labor alongside other disciples who differ in gifting.

Eli Gardner

The role of the local church in making disciples should be the key mission for the body of believers. In the Great Commission found in Matthew 28:18-20, Jesus tells the disciples that they are to make other disciples. They are to take what Jesus taught them over the course of the last three years and teach those very things to others. These teachings, which were recorded for us in the Bible, have been passed down from generation to generation through faithful men and women who were following the great commission. It falls on the leaders of each local church to use their gifts in equipping the saints for the work of the ministry. The end goal of this ministry being making disciples.

Sean Russell

First, if the local church is comprised of local believers, and each of those believers is called to the Great Commission, then the local church's role in disciple-making is and should be a focused effort of Christ's command given to us all in Matt. 28:19-20. While there are many other verses detailing how we are to live the Christian life and edify others, this verse is as simple as it gets. If we can agree that Matt. 28:19-20 is a command to all men and women under Christ's authority, then we should be able to draw from other scriptures and the apostle's examples that prove our collective efforts are not only more effective but necessary for the will of God to unfold, including making disciples.

The book of Titus is a wonderful example of this. Paul gives direct and succinct instructions to Titus on how to operate the local church throughout the island of Crete. Paul is not commanding that Titus take on this daunting task himself, but instead, Titus is to raise up elders, overseers, and women for specific purposes of training others in the

Gospel through their specific roles (disciple-making). The strategy Paul paints is a concerted rather than rogue effort of disciple-making, which should be the goal of our local churches.

CHAPTER 45

Why isn't Discipling More Emphasized in the Church?

"The first cause of the low estate of discipleship
is that pastors have been diverted from their primary calling
to 'equip the saints for the work of the ministry.'"
Greg Ogden[76]

This question may come from someone attending a church where being a disciple isn't emphasized. Perhaps he simply doesn't hear the specific word. There can be many such churches, but no one knows for sure the percentage in America. Or they might hear a sermon as I did once at a U.S. Air Force Chapel, where the chaplain said, "Being a disciple is just too hard for most of us."

Many churches get distracted from their primary purpose: making disciples. To quote Dr. Billie Hanks, "Many pastors and staff members find themselves totally absorbed in a multitude of good activities to the exclusion of the best."[77]

When I was in the military in Europe, I served on the parish council for an Army chapel. There was a monthly meeting with leaders from all the chapel ministries. Each leader would report on

---

[76] Greg Ogden. *Transforming Discipleship: Making Disciples a Few at a Time* (Downers Grove, IL: IVP Books, 2003), 40.

[77] Billie Hanks and William Shell. *Discipleship: Great Insights from the Most Experienced Disciple Makers*. Grand Rapids, MI, Zondervan Publishing House, 1993, 25-26.

what happened in the last month and what was on the schedule for the next. They also projected major expenses and submitted requests for funds. Two things were of primary importance each month: the programs and their attendance counts.

By the time I finished my eight years of duty, I had been on three chapel councils on two Army posts and an Air Force base. There was one thing in common with them all, beyond the program focus. No one ever talked about disciples! They just assumed that every activity would contribute to military members becoming disciples. That was a bad assumption.

It's not much different in a civilian church. They may not have a council of ministry leaders. Many do have an elder or deacon board. One might think that this board would focus on disciple-making. Let me insert a quotation to shed some light on the "why" part of the question above:

> "Elders lead the church, teach and preach the Word, protect the church from false teachers, exhort and admonish the saints in sound doctrine, visit the sick and pray, and judge doctrinal issues. In biblical terminology, elders shepherd, oversee, lead, and care for the local church."[78] [Note: I removed the many Bible citations to shorten this quote.]

Go back and read that again, and this time underline the word disciple. Couldn't find it, could you? Elders, deacons, and pastors have a lot on their plates. Somehow, there doesn't seem to be room for making disciples. Or perhaps, we assume that sound doctrine will result in disciple-making. Bad assumption!

Let me add that I am aware that there are churches that do focus on making disciples. There are a lot of churches that say they do, but some press much more strongly into it. They do more than write a mission statement that includes making disciples. They also ask each ministry to show how they are contributing to disciple-making through an annual evaluation process.

Some churches have a pastor who focuses on disciple-making in the church. Many of them have the word "discipleship" in their titles. They oversee most of the church's discipleship programs. That might include Sunday School, small groups, the men's morning study. Unfortunately, these things don't result in fully-equipped disciples.

---

[78] This quotation is made by Matt Perman in the article "What Is the Role of an Elder?" on the *Desiring God* website. Accessed on June 8, 2019 at: https://www.desiringgod.org/articles/what-is-the-role-of-an-elder

Instead, they tend to focus on teaching "sound doctrine" that doesn't result in making disciples.

It shouldn't come as a surprise that some things fall through the cracks. Elders and pastors have a lot to manage. There are a plethora of expectations put on them by church members. There's that reason again; "That's what we pay them to do." (Although, most elders don't get paid!)

I sat with my senior pastor for an afternoon a few years ago. A seminary course required me to interview a pastor for a seminary course I was doing. He told me that I only got in to see him because one of the other pastors was preaching that week. It amazed me when he shared all the things that he does in a 50-hour workweek. Things were going on behind the scenes, of which I had no idea.

And that's why church members need to face the fact that disciple-making belongs to them. Not to the pastor, not the elders or deacons, or any other leadership role you want to throw in the mix. Making disciples is *your* job. Becoming a disciple is your job. God won't let you point to church leaders as the reason you didn't cut the snuff!

Can the local church emphasize disciple-making more? Sure, they can. But to do that, they might have to give up one of those golden calves that the "squeaky wheel" has been demanding. I would suggest that you might get behind your pastor and help lift some of that burden off his shoulders. And in the meantime, commit to making a disciple regardless of your church's focus.

You may find that disciple-making can go viral through you to many others. Let that be *your* emphasis!

Pastoral Responses

Pierce Eaton

Some churches do a marvelous job of emphasizing disciple-making, but most do not. Churches get caught up in misguided pursuits rather than seeking to build a discipling culture. So often pastors and their churches mistake business for effectiveness. They think that they are just one cool event or gathering away from God moving like a tornado through their church and bringing lasting change to all who participate. This results in the pastor and his church putting all their energy toward ineffective events and programs that do not resemble disciple-making. Trust me, this mentality is easy to get swept into as a pastor. The pastor is desiring for his church to grow numerically, so he plans gimmicks that emphasize numerical growth, but in the end, disciple-making is deemphasized. This pastor and his church are misguided. Jesus did not make filling arenas the goal of the church, he made disciple-making the goal of the church. Of course, pastors should desire growth in their church, but it should not come at the expense of disciple-making. I think pastors, most often, get swept into this misguided pursuit because they neglect their personal call to make disciples.

Your pastor has two callings. He has a calling to lead your church as its pastor (which is a lot of work!), but he also has a personal calling to make disciples as a disciple of Jesus. So often, pastors can get so focused on their calling to lead the church that they neglect their personal calling to make disciples. At first, this can go unnoticed. They are still, after all, teaching and leading the church to become disciple-makers. Over time, however, if a pastor loses his personal drive to make disciples, then it will be reflected in the way he leads the church. He slowly stops talking about discipling in his sermons, and the church stops emphasizing it within the small groups. To the pastor, disciple-making stops being a way of life and eventually becomes a five-step program that one of the church deacons teaches on a Wednesday night a few times a year. Or worse, disciple-making stops being a thing altogether within that church. This is an easy place for a pastor to end up. He has many things on his plate, and disciple-making is not usually a metric by which his church judges his effectiveness, so it often gets neglected. However, there is good news! You can help your pastor by being an agent for building a discipling culture within your local church. I can bet that he would welcome your help in establishing that culture within your church.

Eli Gardner

I believe there are several reasons why discipling is not more emphasized in the church today. The first reason is that many people in the church have never been discipled themselves. Because they have never personally experienced it before, they have no knowledge of what it means nor how it is to be done. The second reason is that it is hard to measure spiritual growth. Counting how many people attend worship, tracking the attendance in small groups, and handing out contribution statements at the end of the year for all that gave is much easier to get numbers for than to track how many read their Bible consistently over the last year. A third reason is that disciple-making is not as flashy as a big event. Doing life with someone else is a lot messier than planning a big event that the community is invited to participate in. A fourth reason is that making disciples can be intimidating. Sitting across from one or two other people and openly sharing information that makes us vulnerable can be a daunting task.

Sean Russell

While I could pontificate for pages, I will keep it to 3 short points. Money, hard work, and goals.

Let's start with money. While all churches face the difficult issue of pleasing man versus God, some churches, unfortunately, have chosen the latter. Bills need to be paid, and many times, the congregants with the largest cash flow are catered to the most. I met with a Navy Chaplain some time ago, and I received some perspective-changing advice. She, too, had previously been a college minister, such as myself, and alerted me to the idea that churches must begin to see college ministry as a missionary type funding. The reason being is this, if we are to raise up our youth and train them properly as disciples, we need to understand that we are investing in kingdom work rather than investing in individuals who can financially invest back. Money, or the lack of it, causes many churches to emphasize the cheap and affordable rather than the costly and effective.

Hard work. Disciple-making isn't pretty. It's not glamorous. It takes long days, extended hours, emotional burden, and simply getting your hands dirty. When we look at the model set by Christ, we see that it took roughly three years of daily walking, teaching, rebuking, reiterating, rescuing, and so forth of 12 men. This is hard enough with one individual, yet Christ was able to take on twelve. With our 40-to-60-hour work weeks, compartmentalization of spirituality, and society/culture grabbing for all our excess attention and money, it is easy to see how we fail at disciple-making. Many simply do not have or are not willing to give their time in this effort.

False Goals. Throughout my time in ministry, one of my biggest pet peeves has been goals, specifically, unrealistic goals. I call them unrealistic because I do not believe that they are biblical, and I believe that by highlighting and focusing on them, we detract from the true mission of disciple-making. For example, I have been a part of events where we were tasked to "guesstimate" how many people we planned on seeing come to faith in Jesus Christ. Now, first of all if we believe that God is sovereign and He is the one who opens the eyes of the heart so that the individual may not only have faith but grace as well (Eph. 2:8-9) then we understand it is not only impossible for us to guess this number but also wrong to even try. The focus has now immediately shifted from a dependency on God to dependency on self (articulation, rhetoric, emotional appeal, etc.) Second, when we focus on this number and set our hopes on it, we are focusing on an arbitrary goal and lose sight of the individual lives at stake. I believe we would all agree that one seed on good soil is better than many scattered on the path, rocky ground, or among weeds. However, the celebration of one individual life is not as well-received as 100 emotional appeals. This model serves as a quick "pump and dump" model where the individual is to be brought to faith and then discarded to figure out the Christian life themselves.

Discipling isn't emphasized enough because it doesn't pay the immediate bills, it's hard work, and we have learned to value the quick and easy.

CHAPTER 46

What Can a Church Do to See More Disciples Made?

"The second cause of the low estate of discipleship
is that we have tried to make disciples through programs."
Greg Ogden[79]

There are several things a church can do to make disciples who then make more disciples. The thing with the most impact is to talk about it from the pulpit. In other words, raise the banner! Books like this one can help a few people get a better vision and begin to grow as disciples. That should be a supplement, not the primary source. The pulpit reaches many more people than this book ever will.

You picked up this book with interest in disciple-making. No one reads a book that they aren't interested in (unless it's for school). Honest questions about discipling must have a source that they come from. If people don't already know about being disciples and making disciples, this book doesn't have a chance.

Things are different in church, though. Most of the time, the churchgoers don't know what the topic of the sermon will be. Maybe your church still puts the sermon title on a sign. But I don't know anyone who decides to attend based on a sermon title. It may be a

---

[79] Greg Ogden. *Transforming Discipleship: Making Disciples a Few at a Time* (Downers Grove, IL: IVP Books, 2003), 42.

sermon series, or a standalone message (whether from random choice or by following a Bible text).

When sermons *regularly* mention being and making disciples, people will begin to embrace the idea. When they hear about the call to be a disciple, they will begin to respond. When they understand what a disciple does, they begin to do that. But this can't be a once a year talk. Isn't it interesting how pastors can give an evangelism call at the end of many sermons, but can't find a way to make a similar call to being a disciple who makes disciples?

Research shows people must hear the gospel 5 to 7 times before they will respond.[80] Most of the baptized need to hear about being a disciple several times before they will grasp the idea. They also need to need to hear about making disciples just as often.

Here's the bottom line. If your church is not talking about being disciples from the pulpit, most people won't become disciples on their own. Those that do become disciples on their own will probably find sources outside the local church.

Your church small groups also need to talk about being disciples who make disciples. And it will be most helpful if they provide clear-cut examples of how to do that. This generally means that these groups need to be led by disciple-makers, not just volunteers. If this doesn't happen, you've got two strikes against you. But there's more that can be done.

Does your church acknowledge high school seniors at the end of the school year? What about mothers on Mother's Day? Veterans on Veteran's Day? How about the birth of a child? Do people clap for a baptism? Each of these things not only endorses the student, mother, or new believer; they also reinforce each action as significant.

Nothing is more momentous than someone becoming a disciple. Or someone who made a disciple.[81] These are the people who are actively pursuing the Great Commission. Why is it that we rarely acknowledge them?

As you think about this, it might seem awkward, maybe even silly. Yet, why do we recognize people for other events but not for

---

[80] See "Sow the Seed" by Tim Blister accessed on June 7, 2019 at: http://timmybrister.com/2011/08/sow-the-seed/ and "Share Jesus Without Fear" accessed on June 7, 2019 at: https://www.allaboutgod.com/share-jesus-without-fear-2.htm

[81] As a young Christian, I thought nothing was more exciting than leading someone to Christ. Until one of those fellows led someone to Christ himself. Whoa; that was mind-blowing!

furthering the kingdom of God? Could it be that we've lost sight of what is most important?

Some people may not like this idea. They might be the ones who need to hear more disciple-making sermons. We cannot stop making disciples because someone values something else, especially if it's distracting from our mission. That's how we got where we are now. We need to obey the Great Commission and help others do the same.

So far, we've talked about emphasizing disciple-making from the pulpit. And about recognizing those who are making disciples. Yet, there's something between these two. We need to provide people with a way to become disciples. And a way to make disciples.

This comes down to putting flesh on the sermons. We now know what a disciple is, and there is some interest, even excitement, in meeting the challenge. Now we need to give them the tools they need to succeed.

I do not intend to promote one program over another. I don't think there is any certain set of materials that will get you completely to your goal. The local church has spent too much time and money trying to replicate another church's success. That church isn't your church.

Instead, a church can evaluate the members who are involved in discipling. How can church leaders measure if someone currently meets the traits of a disciple? (You can't celebrate what you can't measure.) Some will be doing better than others. But you can get an overall sense of where they are as a group. Is something glaringly missing?

Pick that missing trait or some traits that will get the most people closer to being a disciple. Develop a sermon series around that. (Remember that one sermon won't kick things into high gear.) Start a Sunday School class that helps them grow in those areas – one at a time. Have a verse of the month that you ask each member to memorize. A church I visited in Indiana gave a copy of a book to every member. Not only that, the pastor set up a social media page to get maximum involvement.

Think about who is already in your church. Identify a handful of people who already meet the profile of a disciple. Or come close! Start a small group to help them learn how to invest in others. You may have to free them from distractions. Develop them as your first group of disciple-makers. It can be as simple as meeting over coffee to help them work out the details.

Gear your training toward being a disciple and making disciples. And please, keep it simple and focused. I know a church that has a one-year leadership program. People must complete the training before they can lead a small group. There are many helpful subjects in the program. There is also a test that they must pass. It included a question about what was in the Ark of the Covenant. I wasn't clear how that helps lead a group of growing disciples.

A pastor might be able to do most of the above ideas immediately. But a non-formal leader within the church can also do them. You can start a small training group for these leaders and teach them the basics of being a disciple.[82] It's a great first step!

I have heard some people say that they are not allowed to start a small group without their church's permission. My old friend and distance mentor, Skip Gray, had a saying that might apply here: "Smile. Be gracious. Do the will of God." *If* you get kicked out of a church for making disciples, you were in the wrong church. (I've never known anyone to get kicked out for this!)

I put together a small notebook to help me. I'm talking about a field note-sized booklet. In it, I wrote the title of a basic that I want to teach someone else. I have a list of certain Bible verses related to that topic. I also have a list of other materials that I could use if those few verses didn't do the trick. (I keep those extras on "the cloud" for easy access and can even email them to my emerging disciple.)

I stole that idea from a book by LeRoy Eims! *The Lost Art of Disciple Making* has an appendix that lists similar basics to teach to someone.[83] Since the book is over forty years old, I had to update some things to make relevant. You could do the same. You can use that field book with someone from your church, work, or neighborhood.

This little notebook is reproducible. By that, I mean that others can use it—because it's simple. I've had guys borrow it so they can copy everything into a book of their own. And the newest generation of disciplers who simply take photos of each page to access on their phones. Either way, that results in more disciples who make disciples!

---

[82] For a simple list of basics that you can start with "Seven Basics to Develop in Those You Disciple" by Justin Gravitt. Accessed on June 7, 2019 at: https://www.justingravitt.com/blog/7basics

[83] LeRoy's book is no longer in print. You either need to get a used copy or, as of June 2019, it's still available as an ebook for purchase.

Pastoral Responses

Pierce Eaton

So often, we want a simple reproducible process that we can implement in a church to "fix" whatever "problem" we might have. Disciple-making is no different. Many pastors and church leaders seek out a perfect five-step program that leads to disciples being made in their church, but that perfect program eludes them. This is because building a discipling culture within a church is not a step by step process. It isn't a program or class that can be taught in a few weeks. Leading a church to a place where it sees more disciples being made is much simpler than one might think.

For most churches, all they must do to see an increase in disciple making is to emphasize disciple making. I know, that seems too simple. But to reiterate one of Bruce's statements, emphasizing disciple-making is much more than simply bringing it up in a sermon once a year. The pastor should find ways of incorporating the language of disciple-making into his sermons regularly. This doesn't mean that he must preach on the great commission every week or that disciple-making must be the complete focus of every sermon. Rather, he simply needs to help the congregation see how the primary point of his sermon applies to being and making disciples. By implementing this emphasis, a pastor can give challenges on disciple-making to the church weekly.

Likewise, the small groups in the church also need to have a disciple-making emphasis. This does not mean that every week the group must go through a curriculum that covers disciple-making. Instead, you can take the curriculum that your church already uses and begin trying to incorporate disciple-making into the conversation. The more a church begins to talk about being and making disciples, the more that congregation begins to see life through the disciple making lens. As people begin to see life through the disciple making lens, they begin making disciples.

If you are not a pastor or church leader, you can still greatly impact the disciple-making of your church. The best way to do that is to seek to impact your sphere of influence first. You likely have a group of people at your church that you are close with. Maybe they are the people in your small group or the people you regularly sit with on a Sunday morning. You can start to change the discipling culture of your church by seeking to impact that group. Begin talking about being and making disciples with that group. Seek to mentor and teach those people how to make disciples.

Every person in your sphere of influence has their own sphere of influence that will be different than yours. If you impact the people in your sphere of influence for disciple-making, then they will begin to impact the people in their sphere of influence and so-on. Before long, many of the people in your church will have become infected by the disciple-making bug you helped to put in your friends or small group. Disciple-making is contagious, and you can be "patient-zero" in your church.

Eli Gardner

A church can do several things to see more disciples made. First, it's best if the pastor gets onboard with the vision of disciple-making. When he becomes the chief disciple-maker and encourager of others making disciples, then more people in the church will catch on and will follow suit. Secondly, it begins with one person seeing the vision and meeting with a small group for training and vision casting. If you start big, it will fail big. If you start slow, it will grow. Once this small group is trained, then they will be able to start their own groups while the leader starts with a new group once again. And third, be patient. Disciple-making does not happen overnight, nor does immediately it change the culture of a church. It's messy, but it's worth it.

Sean Russell

While I could make a list, I will simply say that the church needs to put their money where their mouth is. Invest in programs that do not have a quick financial yield. Invest in people and groups that specifically work on training disciples rather than catering to the masses. Invest money in a way that honors Christ yet confounds the world.

Too often, our churches want to be culturally relevant, and this causes them to allocate kingdom dollars to worldly means. We need to commit ourselves to people and programs that will raise up a generation of true followers of Christ. If this occurs, we wouldn't have to worry about mass amounts of people to get the missions done. We could simply repeat the model where 12 individuals changed the world through the training of Jesus Christ, the power of the Holy Spirit, and the will of God.

In Closing

My hope, my prayer, my overwhelming desire is that you have gotten answers to honest questions about being a disciple and making disciples. And that these real answers have helped you learn how to make disciples and have removed any obstacles and distractions. And that you have been motivated to be a disciple who makes disciples from this book.

My goal is that this book, and my other books about discipling, will result in 20,000 people discipling one other person over the next three years. As each discipler helps another person arrive at the point of a full-fledged disciple, we will begin to see them reach others. But that's not the end goal.

The end goal is not for three years but is at least 15 years out. I expect by then to have run my race and be close to the finish line. Yet in years four through six, there will be 40,000 more growing disciples. In years seven through nine, 80,000 more. And 160,000 more in years ten through twelve. Finally, in years thirteen through fifteen, as a mighty movement of God, we will see 320,000 more disciples who will make disciples.

Fifteen years from now, if God gives that time to me, I hope to have contributed to the making of over a half-million disciples who make disciples! From there, each of you will continue to fulfill the Great Commission of Jesus Christ of making disciples who make disciples in every nation/people group found on Earth.

As you finish this book and sit it on a shelf, I want to continue to contribute to your disciple-making adventure. If I can count on you as a disciple who makes disciples, please drop me a message on my Facebook page, Bruce Stopher - Author. You can also join the Facebook Group Disciples Who Make Disciples and interact with other people across the globe who are striving to be disciples who make disciples.

Until the day when we all gather around the throne and sing our praises to the Lamb, I humbly ask you to commit to being a disciple who makes disciples.

~

And some final details.

Thank you for buying this book! You can help get the word out about *Disciples Who Make Disciples*.

If you found this book helpful, would you please consider writing a review on Amazon and/or Goodreads? An honest review of at least 100 words is most helpful for other people ("I loved it" isn't usually helpful). Using keywords like "disciple" and "disciple-making" in your review will help others find this book on Amazon. Your review will help others get their questions answered and perhaps propel an even larger disciple-making movement!

Also, you can follow me on Facebook at Bruce Stopher – Author. I post small portions of any book I'm currently writing there, and you can review and offer suggestions before it's even printed!

Free Offer to My Readers

I am fully committed to being a disciple, and to making disciples who make disciples. I personally help people who live near me become disciple-makers. But I also want to help people to become disciple-makers no matter where they are.

To help you do that. I want to offer a free resource to you. I am actively working on another book that will give you step-by-step help to follow-up a new Christian, or a Christian who has never been followed-up. While there will be a print version of this book, there will also be an ebook version. That ebook version will be free to anyone on my *Disciples Who Make Disciples* email list.

Occasionally, I will offer other resources from this email list, but you will not receive an email more than once a month.

To get your free copy of the ebook, enter your email address at: https://tinyurl.com/disciplemaker

Appendix

Other Opinions of the Definition of a Disciple?

"Should you ask ten different people in the church
(including the pastoral staff) what a disciple is,
you might get ten different answers.
The same is true at a seminary.
If the church is not clear on what Jesus meant,
then it will be difficult to comply with his expressed will."
Aubrey Malphurs[84]

In Part Three of this book, I asked some pastors for input on my answers about the local church and disciple-making. To be fair, I also want to give some input from other people on the definition of a disciple. Several other people whom I greatly respect have addressed the traits of a disciple. So below, you will find some quotations that include the characteristics of a disciple. I would suggest that you compare the traits of a disciple given here to those in chapter eight.

~

Gene Warr (1924-2006) was a phenomenal man. I was privileged to hear him speak on several occasions across Texas. He served in General Patton's Third Army during World War II and left the Army in 1946 having achieved the rank of Captain. Gene gave his life to Christ in 1947 while he was working with his father in Oklahoma developing land, including the city of Warr Acres in the metro area of Oklahoma City.

Gene was considered the spiritual father of the Navigator ministry in Oklahoma City, and although he was never on staff with The Navigators, many Navigators point to him as the foundation of their Christian training. You can listen to many of Gene's messages stored at DiscipleshipLibrary.com. He wrote several books, as did his wife Irma, and the following is Gene's description of a disciple:

---

[84] Aubrey Malphurs. *Strategic Disciple Making: A Practical Tool for Successful Ministry* (Grand Rapids: Baker Books, 2009), 18.

A disciple has been born again; loves God; is a learner; lives under the authority of Jesus Christ; abides in the Word of God; loves the household of faith; bears fruit; is willing to forsake people; positively identified with Christ; and must be willing to forsake his possessions [ten bullet points condensed by me].[85]

~

Francis Cosgrove (life details unknown) was on Director of Church Relations for The Navigators at the time (1980) he wrote two books on the essentials of the Christian Life. I was only able to hear Francis speak once in Colorado. This was a man who not only gave his life to making disciples, but also left a great legacy in the lives of many men across the United States. Here is his biblical profile of a disciple:

A disciple is a learner—open and teachable; puts Christ first in all areas of his life; is committed to a life of purity; has a devotional time and is developing his prayer life; demonstrates faithfulness and a desire to learn and apply the Word of God; has a heart for witnessing and presents the gospel regularly; attends church regularly and makes a contribution to the body; displays love and unity; demonstrates a servant's heart; gives regularly and honors God with his finances; demonstrates the fruit of the spirit [eleven bullet points condensed by me].[86]

~

Ron Kincaid was the pastor of Sunset Presbyterian Church in Portland, Oregon when he wrote a book in 1990 on disciple-making in the church, and he is still the senior pastor there (as of 2019). His definition of a disciple was very simple:

"A disciple is someone who learns from Christ and is following Christ."[87]

---

[85] Gene Warr. *Making Disciples* (Oklahoma City: Temple Press, 1990), 52.

[86] Francis M. Cosgrove Jr. *Essentials of Discipleship: Practical Help on How to Live as Christ's Disciple* (Colorado Springs: Navpress, 1980), 15-16. Francis included three to seven Scripture refences with each profile point he made.

[87] Ron Kincaid. *A Celebration of Disciple-Making* (Wheaton: Victor Books, 1990), 17.

Aubrey Malphurs is professor of pastoral ministries at Dallas Theological Seminary. I had one occasion to hear him speak, although it was not on the topic of disciple-making. This appendix opened with a quote from him implying that without a solid definition of a disciple, the local church will have difficulty obeying Christ's Great Commission. His definition follows:

"I contend that the normative use of the term disciple is for one who is a convert to or a believer in Jesus Christ. Thus the Bible teaches that a disciple is not necessarily a Christian who has made a deeper commitment to the Savior but simply a Christian. Committed Christians are committed disciples. Uncommitted Christians are uncommitted disciples."[88]

---

[88] Aubrey Malphurs. *Strategic Disciple Making: A Practical Tool for Successful Ministry* (Grand Rapids: Baker Books, 2009), 18.

Glossary

Basics – a term disciple-makers may use to describe several spiritual practices to help a person grow in a relationship with God and as a disciple. At a minimum, these include the lordship of Jesus and obedience to him, a practice of being in the Word and prayer (the foundations of a relationship with Christ), and growing in relationship with others who are fellow believers (fellowship) or non-Christians (witnessing).

Church – This word is used with two meanings. When the word is capitalized (Church), it means the entire body of Christ on Earth. Adverbs used to describe the Church include catholic, triumphant, universal, and worldwide. The catholic church is not the same as the Roman Catholic Church – a denomination. The Church consists of believers in every country, some of whom cannot attend a meeting without risk of death. When the word is not capitalized (church) it means the local church gathered in a neighborhood. This local church may contain people who are not yet Christians.

Community – Community can have two meanings. The most common use refers to a neighborhood or small region, normally smaller than a town. But among Christians, community is also a synonym for fellowship but can be narrow than a group of people having a major trait in common. Often among Christians, community refers to a small group of fellow believers who are actively engaged in each other's lives.

Disciple – as a noun, a Christian who is growing in his walk with Christ by following him, denying himself, carrying a personal cross, abiding in the Word, and bearing fruit – both in his character and through other people coming to Christ and beginning to grow in their faith.

Disciple – as a verb, to disciple someone is to intentionally invest in key traits that will result in that person becoming a disciple. It may begin with following up on someone coming to faith in Christ, yet it focuses primarily on helping him develop the traits of a disciple listed in chapter eight of this book. Mentor and coach are actions that can take place simultaneously but may not contribute to achieving the traits of a disciple. It has a final goal that should be attained within a few years and maintained for the rest of one's earthly life.

Disciple-maker – the general term means anyone who has helped another person become a disciple. There is a strong assumption that a disciple-maker must already be a disciple and is intentional in helping another person develop in the traits of a disciple.

Discipler – a person who is beginning to help a new or immature believer in the basics of the Christian life. Following-up on his decision to embrace salvation through faith by grace and begin to be established in a walk led by the Holy Spirit.

Emerging Disciple – I use this term to describe a young-in-faith Christian who is beginning to grow in his walk with Christ toward being a disciple. He may not have acquired all the traits of a disciple noted in Section One, but he is moving toward them with the help of a disciple-maker.

Follow-up – a precursor to disciple-making, follow-up describes the initial activity of helping a new believer become established in his faith. Follow-up addresses the basics of the Christian walk, including areas such as assurance of salvation, developing a prayer life, reading the Bible, fellowshipping with other believers, and letting friends and family know about his new faith.

Laymen – a term often used in a church setting that differentiates the common church member from the clergy (ordained ministers). In the Bible, the Apostle Paul often called these people "saints" (Ephesians 1:1; Philippians 1:1; and Colossians 1:2).

Ministry – any work that is done within a church that leads to the maturity of others (Ephesians 4:7-16), as shown by the servant leadership of Jesus Christ. Disciple-making, whether done by one person or corporately, focuses on this maturity outcome. Many Christians today also see ministry as reaching into the community surrounding the church.

Personal Devotions – this includes other terms like "quiet time" and "time alone with God." A devotional time is a time set aside during the day for personal Bible reading and prayer. The focus of a devotional time is to spend time in relationship with God, hearing him through the Scriptures and responding from the heart. Some people journal their thoughts during these times.

Synoptic Gospels – A term Bible scholars give to the Gospels of Matthew, Mark, and Luke that are said to each take a common view of the story of Jesus with slight variations. The Gospel of John is different from these three in its limited time-frame yet expanded depth in the final weeks of Jesus' personal ministry.

ABOUT THE AUTHOR

Bruce "Bruder" Stopher

While I was born in Chicago, Illinois, my family moved from place to place until I finished high school in Minnesota. I joined the U.S. Army and arrived at my first duty station: Fort Knox, Kentucky. It was there that I came to fully understand the gospel, which I had heard from early childhood. I was then discipled by a bank teller from the Fort Knox National Bank. Countless others would invest in me over the next 45 years. I also began to learn how to disciple others.

After eight years of active duty, I moved to San Antonio, Texas. I put my G.I. Bill to work and earned a nursing degree (BSN) from UT Health. I continued to grow in my discipling skills since then. In 1988, I joined the staff of a disciple-making ministry.

I earned a Master of Arts in Religion in Pastoral Studies from Liberty University (2014), followed by a Master of Divinity focusing on Discipleship and Church Ministry (2017). I have an addiction to books with five large bookcases filled to overflowing, along with a Kindle that required a larger memory card! I am a widower, due to breast cancer, with three adult children in three different states.

You may contact me directly through my Facebook *Bruce Stopher – Author* page.

Made in the USA
Las Vegas, NV
09 September 2021